# Inhalt

# Unit 1 Australia

## 1 Welcome to Australia! ▸ *pp. 6–7*

*Read Judith's blog on pp. 6–7 of your student's book and complete the sentences in your own words.*

*1* In the plane Judith felt very small and a bit scared because she saw how huge Australia was.

*2* When Judith landed in Melbourne she felt cold because ______________________

*3* School in Australia is different from school in Germany because ______________________

*4* During a 5-day hike in the bush, something really scary happened. Before Judith went to bed one night, ______________________

*5* In their free time, lots of Australian teenagers ______________________

### ●* Now you

*Read again what Judith says about school life and free time for teenagers in Australia. What's different from Germany? Find four differences. Make notes first. Then write about 60–80 words in your exercise book.*

While Australia is cold in July, Germany can be hot. In Australia ..., but in Germany ...

## ○** 2 WORDS Australia puzzle ▸ *pp. 6–7*

**a)** *Complete with words from pp. 6–7.*

*1* Another name for Australia is ...

*2* Australia's huge area of dry[1] land is called the ...

*3* In Australia from June to August it's ...

*4* A 'barbie' in Australia is a ...

*5* The river that Melbourne stands on is the ...

*6* Melbourne is in the state of ...

*7* Everybody's favourite Australian animal is the ...

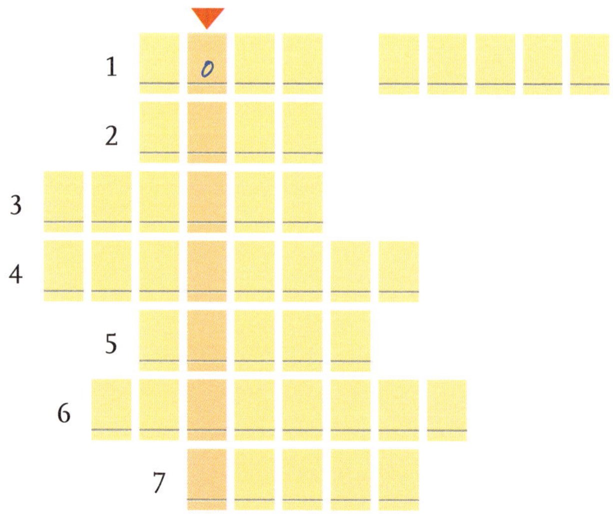


**b)** *The word in the orange boxes is another name for 2 in a):*

0202 the o ______________________

[1] dry [draɪ] *trocken*

## 3 Australia Quiz

▸ pp. 8–9

*a) Look at pp. 8–9 of your student's book again. Then tick answer A, B or C. You need the letters in brackets in b).*

1 The capital of Australia is … A Melbourne. (P) B Canberra. (G) C Sydney. (D)

2 There are … stars on the Australian flag. A eight (M) B five (P) C six (O)

3 The first Europeans landed in Australia in the … century. A 14th (G) B 15th (I) C 16th (E)

4 In 1788 the British started a colony in Port Jackson for …
A farmers. (L) B prisoners. (R) C Native Americans. (E)

5 The Commonwealth of Australia was founded in … A 1770. (S) B 1788. (T) C 1901. (B)

6 Which animals are only found in Australia?
A Emu, lion, kangaroo. (U) B Koala, emu, kangaroo. (A) C Koala, kangaroo, lion. (L)

7 The Great Barrier Reef is famous for its …
A good surfing. (O) B birds. (H) C corals. (S)

8 The Great Barrier Reef is … long.
A more than 200 km (N) B 1,500 km (H) C 200 miles (F)

9 A big health problem for the people of Australia is …
A crime in the cities. (M) B the hole in the ozone layer. (I) C the cane toad. (E)

10 Today most immigrants to Australia come from …
A the USA. (O) B Asia. (I) C Britain. (E)

*b) Write down the letters in brackets after your answers. If your answers are correct, you can put the letters in the right order to give you the name of a group of people:* ______________________

*c) Use the information on p. 8 of your student's book to complete the timeline of Australian history. Use the simple present.*

| 16th century | 1770 | ________ | 1788–1868 | ________ |
|---|---|---|---|---|
| The first ships arrive from ________ ________ | Captain James Cook ________ ________ | A colony for prisoners is founded in Port Jackson. | ________ ________ ________ ________ | Australia becomes independent. |

## 4 REVISION The emu (Simple present)

▸ p. 11 • GF (p. 159)

*Find out some facts about the emu (from books or the internet), for example, what it does and doesn't do, how long it lives, what it eats or how fast it can run. Write a short text in the simple present in your exercise book.*

0304 *The emu only lives in Australia. It's a large bird that doesn't fly …*

## 5 REVISION A famous Australian (Simple past) ▸ p. 11 • GF (p. 160)

*a) Write the verbs in the correct form.*

Australian movie star Cate Blanchett _was_ (be) born in Melbourne in 1969. She _went_ (go) to drama school in Sydney, then ______ (work) in theatre and TV. She ______ (~~become~~) an international star until 1998, when she ______ (play) Queen Elizabeth I of England in the film *Elizabeth*. She was nominated for an Oscar as Best Actress, but she ______ (~~win~~) that year. From 2001 she ______ (take) the role of queen Galadriel in the three parts of *The Lord of the Rings*. Then in 2005 she ______ (win) an Oscar for her role in *The Aviator* with Leonardo DiCaprio. In 2008 she ______ (get) a star on the Hollywood *Walk of Fame*, and in 2009 she ______

0405 (appear) on two Australian postage stamps[1].

*b) Prepare a biography of another famous Australian for a two-minute talk in class. Use the simple past.*

Ideas: Nicole Kidman • Mel Gibson • Russell Crowe • Kylie Minogue • Lleyton Hewitt

## 6 Extra STUDY SKILLS Charts ▸ p. 11 • SF (p. 140)

*Write about the two charts. What kind of charts are they? What do they show? Give details and a conclusion. Use phrases from your student's book (p. 10): e. g. this is a pie/bar chart, it shows ..., it is divided into ... sections, the largest group is ... Write about chart 2 in your exercise book.*

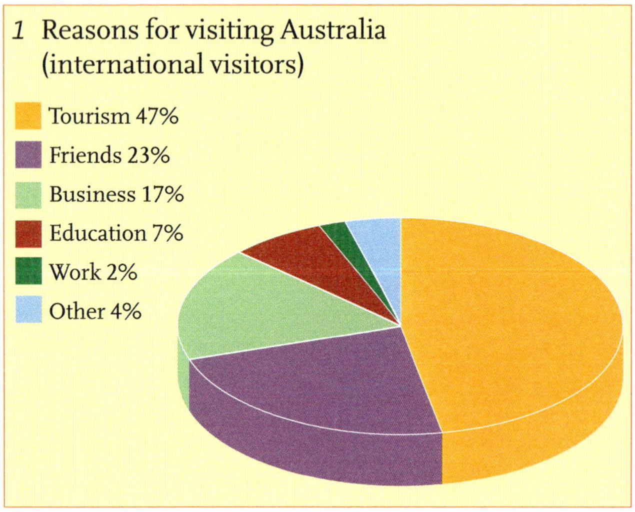


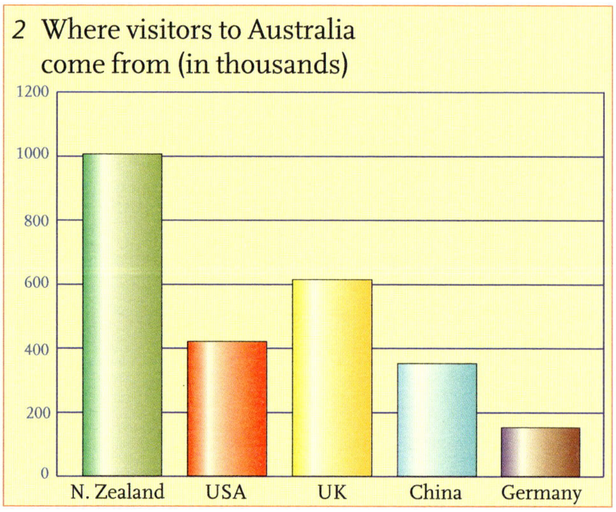


(Source: Travel Research Australia, 2009)

1 _This is a ______ . It shows what percentage of international visitors go to Australia for what reasons. It is divided into six ______

______

______

______

______

[1]postage stamp ['pəʊstɪdʒ stæmp] *Briefmarke*

## 7 EVERYDAY ENGLISH WRITING An e-mail

▸ p. 14 • WB (pp. 74–75) • SF (p. 153)

*You would like to know more about the Alice Springs School of the Air. Write an e-mail to Jeannie in your exercise book and ask her how it works. Here are some notes. You can add your own ideas. Think of a good closing sentence too.*

Ideas: when – school – start and finish? • how many/long – lessons? • which/how many – school subjects? • when/how – homework, tests? • school grades?

Dear Jeannie,
I found your e-mail really interesting. I'd like to know more about the School of the Air, so maybe you can answer my questions.
First, when does school ...

WB, pp. 59–62

## 8 EVERYDAY ENGLISH MEDIATION

### Climbing Sydney Harbour Bridge (Spoken English to German)

▸ p. 14 • WB (p. 76) 🎧 2

**a)** *You are going to climb Sydney Harbour Bridge with your family. You call the Bridge hotline to find out answers to your parents' questions. Read the questions first. Then listen carefully to your CD (🎧 2) and take notes in German.*

1 Wie kommt man am besten zur Brücke?

2 Kann man mit dem Auto hinfahren?

3 Wann müssen wir dort sein?

4 Gibt es für die Teilnehmer/innen eine Vorbereitung?

5 Wie lange dauert der Aufstieg?

6 Gibt es Dinge, die wir nicht tun dürfen?

7 Was soll man anziehen?

8 Was geschieht, wenn das Wetter schlecht ist?

**INFO BOX**

When Sydney Harbour Bridge was opened in 1932, it was used by about 11,000 cars every day. Now the average is more than 150,000 cars a day!

WB, pp. 65–66

**b)** *Answer your parents' questions.*

## 9 LISTENING Captain James Cook ▸ p. 14 • WB (p. 71) 3

Test

*a) Listen to the short biography of James Cook. While you listen the first time, take notes about dates and main facts in your exercise book. Then listen again and tick the right box. The words at the bottom of the page will help you.*

| | True | False | Not in the text |
|---|---|---|---|
| 1 James was born in Scotland. | | ✔ | |
| 2 His mother was from Yorkshire. | | | |
| 3 After school James became a farm worker like his father. | | | |
| 4 He started to work for a shipowner when he was 17. | | | |
| 5 He worked hard and learned a lot to become a good navigator[1]. | | | |
| 6 He started his first journey to the Pacific Ocean in 1770. | | | |
| 7 His first ship was called the *Resolution*. | | | |
| 8 He claimed[2] Australia for Britain on his first Pacific journey. | | | |
| 9 The British Navy[3] paid him well because he was an excellent navigator. | | | |
| 10 Cook was a very good map maker. | | | |
| 11 He was killed in Australia. | | | |

WB, pp. 50–53

*b) In one sentence, write why James Cook is famous in British history.*

---

## 10 WORDS Explaining words ▸ p. 14

*Match the sentence parts and add **who**, **which/that** or **where** to make correct definitions.*

| | |
|---|---|
| A teenager is | a person ______ saves swimmers from the sea if they are in danger. |
| A couch potato is | a person *who* ______ is over 12 but not yet 20 years old. |
| A desert is | something ______ you put on your skin to protect it from the sun. |
| Sunscreen is | a hot place ______ people don't live and trees don't grow. |
| A witness is | a person ______ likes to stay at home and watch TV. |
| A lifeguard is | a person ______ sees an accident or a crime and can describe what happened. |

0610

[1] navigator ['nævɪgeɪtə] *Seefahrer* [2] claim [kleɪm] *in Besitz nehmen* [3] Navy ['neɪvi] *Marine*

## 11 SPEAKING COURSE Part 1: Excuse me, … (Having a conversation)

▸ p. 15 • WB (pp. 72–73) 4

a) *Mark the phrases you could use in the different steps of a conversation. There is more than one correct answer.*

**Step 1**: You want to start a conversation with somebody you don't know.

Excuse me, … • Do you like …? • Hi! • Nice to meet you.

**Step 2**: You introduce yourself.

Bye! • I'm … by the way. • Why don't you …? • My name's … • Nice to meet you.

**Step 3**: You start with small talk and a few general questions.

Have you ever … ? • See you later. • Are you from here? • Can I borrow …?

**Step 4**: You ask for help or information.

Can you tell me …? • How are you doing? • Do you know where …? • See you tomorrow.

**Step 5**: You end the conversation.

Bye! • Great weather today. • See you later, maybe. • Have a good day! • Thanks for your help.

b) *Ben, a student from the UK, wants to go to Bondi Beach, so he asks a girl on the street where he can buy some things that he needs. Complete the conversation with phrases from a). More than one answer is possible.*

*Ben* Hi! Excuse me, …

*Girl* Hi! Going to the beach?

*Ben* Yes, but it's a bit too hot for me.

____________________

*Girl* Hi, Ben! I'm Lucy. Nice ____________ . You're from the UK, right?

*Ben* Yes, I am. From London.

____________________ ?

*Girl* Sure. I've lived here all my life. It's a great city.

*Ben* This is my first day here. I didn't think it would be so hot. ____________

____________________ I can get some sunscreen and a hat?

*Girl* Sure. There's a place that sells tourist stuff just round the corner, that way. Then you can slip, slop, slap. (*laughing*) That's what we do here – because of the sun. 'Slip! Slop! Slap!' Get sunsmart. You'll learn.

0711
0712

*Ben* Mmm? Oh. Well, ____________ . ____________

*Girl* ____________ , maybe. ____________

c) *Now listen to the CD (4) and check your answers. The CD gives only one possible answer. Then listen again and read out the dialogue with your CD.*

WB, pp. 63–64

d) *Write a new dialogue between Ben, who now wants to rent a bike for the day, and a girl he meets on the beach. Use phrases from the five steps in a) and ideas from b).*

## 12 WORDS Word families ▸ p. 17

*a) Fill in the missing words.*

| Verb | Noun | Adjective |
|---|---|---|
| — | Aborigine | Aboriginal |
| surprise | ______ | surprised, surprising |
| advise | ______ | — |
| — | race | ______ |
| ______ | apology | — |
| believe | ______ | — |
| — | history | ______ |

*b) Use words from a) in the correct form to complete the sentences.*

1 It's important to respect the traditions and ______ of the Aborigines.

2 At Uluru there are signs which ______ visitors not to climb the rock.

3 Thousands of Aboriginal children were taken from their families because of the government's ______ policy. The government didn't ______ until 2008.

0812 4 The film *Rabbit-proof fence* describes true, ______ facts about the 'stolen generations'.

## 13 Climbing Uluru (Indirect speech) ▸ p. 19 • WB (p. 76)

*You asked two Australian teenagers about climbing Uluru. What did they tell you?*

1 Uluru is unbelievable. If you go there, you'll never forget it.
2 I have a friend who has climbed it.
3 But it isn't like other rocks that tourists climb.

4 The Aborigines don't want people to climb Uluru.
5 It's against their culture and visitors have to respect that.
6 I hope we'll go to Uluru again, but we won't climb it.

1 The girl said that *Uluru was unbelievable, and that if I went there, I would never forget it.*

2 She said that she ______

3 She added that it ______

4 The boy explained that ______

5 He said that ______

0813 6 He hoped that ______

## 14 WRITING My favourite film

▸ p. 19 • WB (pp. 74–75)

**a)** *Complete the text about your favourite film in your exercise book with your own words.*

The title of my favourite film is '…' It's … (*a comedy, a love story, an adventure film …*). The stars of the film are … The story takes place in … (*place and time*). It's about … The main characters are … The action is … (*funny, slow, fast …*) and the soundtrack is … (*fantastic, brilliant …*).

WB, pp. 59–62

**b)** *In your exercise book, add sentences about the* ***special effects*** *and about the* ***ending****. Say why you would* ***recommend*** *the film.*

## 15 READING WORKING WITH THE TEXT In the outback

▸ pp. 20–24 • WB (pp. 71–72)

**a)** *You can find the following words in the story in your student's book (pp. 20–23). How can you work out the meanings? Write A, B, C or D after the words. Sometimes two answers are correct. Then write the German meaning of the word and check your answers with a dictionary.*

| A from a picture | B from the context | C from words I already know | D the word is like a German word |
|---|---|---|---|

| | | | | | |
|---|---|---|---|---|---|
| ute (*line* 19) | *A, B* | *Lieferwagen* | bark (*line* 146) | ___ | ___ |
| inland (*line* 29) | ___ | ___ | boar (*line* 156) | ___ | ___ |
| sandy (*line* 32) | ___ | ___ | bones (*line* 159) | ___ | ___ |
| cut (*line* 120) | ___ | ___ | tusks (*line* 179) | ___ | ___ |
| pour (*line* 121) | ___ | ___ | stick (*line* 203) | ___ | ___ |
| salty (*line* 128) | ___ | ___ | wound (*line* 231) | ___ | ___ |

**b)** *Complete the sentences with true facts from the story. Use your own words.*

1 Bill, Colm and Rusty are in the outback because *it's Bill's job to repair the Dog Fence.*

2 One day something is wrong with Rusty, but ______

3 Colm shoots the black boar because ______

4 After the attack, Colm knows that he has to ______

5 Colm has to run to Tara Downs because ______

WB, pp. 54–58

6 Colm doesn't want to lie in bed in the house because ______

**c)** *Write an e-mail to a friend in your exercise book and tell him/her about the story. Say who is in the story, where it takes place, what the characters are doing and what is the most important event. You can also say how the story makes you feel – sad, nervous, happy. Which part of the story do you find the most exciting? Write at least ten sentences.*

0916 0917

*Hi …! I must tell you about a story that I have just read, about a boy, a man and his dog. It takes place in the Australian outback …*

# Skills Check 1



## 1 LISTENING Summer vacation 5

*You are going to hear a conversation between Dan and his sister, Mel. First read the sentences below. Then listen and tick A, B or C. You will hear the recording twice.*

1 The conversation takes place ...
- A on a train to Brisbane.
- B on a plane to Melbourne.
- C on a bus to Darwin.

2 Their arrival time will be ...
- A 4.45.
- B 14.45.
- C 14.54.

3 Why are Dan and Mel going there?
- A To go to summer camp
- B To do a summer job
- C To visit family

4 Mel and Ruth are ...
- A friends.
- B sisters.
- C cousins.

5 During their vacation Dan and Mel are planning to ...
- A go shopping.
- B do lots of sport.
- C see lots of sights.

6 They have already been to the City Museum ...
- A twice.
- B three times.
- C four times.



## 2 LISTENING A day in the life of ... 6

*You are going to hear part of a radio interview with two firefighters from the Queensland Fire Service. First read the sentences below, then listen to the recording. You will hear the recording twice.*

**a)** *What is the interview about? Tick the correct box.*

- ☐ A koala rescue operation
- ☐ The history of bushfires in Queensland
- ☐ Why bushfires start

**b)** *Tick true or false.*

| | | *True* | *False* |
|---|---|---|---|
| 1 | Bob has been a firefighter for 30 years. | ☐ | ☐ |
| 2 | Steve had an office job with a company before he became a firefighter. | ☐ | ☐ |
| 3 | On average, Queensland gets about 258 days of sunshine a year. | ☐ | ☐ |
| 4 | In the fire season firefighters work round the clock and get very little sleep. | ☐ | ☐ |
| 5 | Bob flies a helicopter with waterbombing equipment. | ☐ | ☐ |
| 6 | Natural causes of bushfires are high temperatures and strong winds. | ☐ | ☐ |
| 7 | Eucalyptus forests burn easily because of the oil in the leaves. | ☐ | ☐ |
| 8 | People can't do anything to prevent[1] bushfires. | ☐ | ☐ |
| 9 | It's often difficult to make people leave their homes, although the fires are close. | ☐ | ☐ |
| 10 | Bob remembers saving a little girl's cat from the garden of her ruined house. | ☐ | ☐ |

[1] prevent [prɪ'vent] *verhindern*

## 3 READING Sydney for everyone

*a) Look at the text quickly. What is it about? Tick a box.*

☐ Sydney's beaches ☐ Sydney's history ☐ Sydney's sights

*b) Look at the text a second time. What information does it give? Tick the correct boxes.*

☐ Opening times ☐ Prices ☐ Sights information ☐ How to get there

### SYDNEY FOR EVERYONE

**Start at The Rocks**

The Rocks is the oldest part of Sydney. It is an area of great historical importance because Sydney was founded here when the first British prisoners arrived in 1788. Because of its colonial buildings it is often called Sydney's 'outdoor museum'. But today The Rocks also has trendy boutiques, souvenir shops, cafés, restaurants and a weekend street market. The Sydney Visitor Centre is here too, so it's a good place to start your walking tour.
**Open** daily from 9.30 am to 5.30 pm.

**Climb Sydney Harbour Bridge**

This is one of Sydney's most popular tourist attractions, called the 'Coat Hanger' by local people. It's easy to see why. Don't miss the challenge[1] of the Bridge Climb. You won't forget it! The building of the bridge took eight years. It was opened in 1932, and it is used by about 150,000 vehicles[2] daily. It takes about 80,000 litres of paint to paint the bridge once, and painting never stops. Did you know that the movie star Paul Hogan, better known as 'Crocodile Dundee', used to be a bridge painter before he became famous? **Opening times**: 7 am to 8 pm daily.

**Visit Sydney's historic buildings**

Visit Elizabeth Farm in Parramatta, the oldest European building in Australia. Begun in 1793, the farm was the home of John and Elizabeth Macarthur, settlers from England who became sheep farmers and started Australia's wool export industry. The old house, its furniture and its gardens show visitors how they lived in the early 19th century. **Open** 9.30 am to 4 pm Fri to Sun.

**See a world-famous sight**

The spectacular Sydney Opera House is situated in Sydney Harbour, surrounded by water on three sides. It was built by a Danish architect and was completed in 1973. Its design is a masterpiece of 20th century architecture and a world-famous sight. By the way, not only opera but also concerts, theatre and ballet are performed here.

**Visit Sydney Aquarium**

Sydney Aquarium is one of the biggest in the world, with at least 6,000 fish, mostly Australian, and 650 different kinds of fish and marine animals. Visitors walk through underwater viewing tunnels to see marine life close up. Don't miss looking a huge shark[3] in the eye!
**Opening times**: 9 am–10 pm daily.

[1] challenge ['tʃæləndʒ] *Herausforderung* [2] vehicle ['viːəkl] *Fahrzeug* [3] shark [ʃɑːk] *Hai*

READING

*c) Is the information true (T), false (F) or not in the text (N)? Tick the correct box.*

| | T | F | N |
|---|---|---|---|
| 1 The Rocks is an area of Sydney which reminds[1] visitors of Australia's colonial history. | ☐ | ☐ | ☐ |
| 2 Prisoners from America arrived there in 1788. | ☐ | ☐ | ☐ |
| 3 Sydney Opera House is near Sydney Harbour on a small island. | ☐ | ☐ | ☐ |
| 4 Tourists love The Rocks farmers' market on Fridays. | ☐ | ☐ | ☐ |
| 5 Sydney Harbour Bridge was started in 1924. | ☐ | ☐ | ☐ |
| 6 The Bridge is a railway bridge only. | ☐ | ☐ | ☐ |
| 7 Painting the Harbour Bridge is a never-ending job. | ☐ | ☐ | ☐ |
| 8 Sydney Aquarium is home to 6,000 kinds of Australian fish. | ☐ | ☐ | ☐ |
| 9 A European architect designed and built Sydney Opera House. | ☐ | ☐ | ☐ |
| 10 The Macarthurs were cattle farmers from England. | ☐ | ☐ | ☐ |
| 11 People call John Macarthur 'the father of the wool industry'. | ☐ | ☐ | ☐ |
| 12 You can also see theatre productions at the Sydney Opera House. | ☐ | ☐ | ☐ |

WRITING

## 4 WRITING An e-mail or a summary

*Complete a) or b).*

*a) You are in Sydney. Write an interesting e-mail to an English friend about a day's sightseeing[2] there (about 100 words). You may take some facts from 'Sydney for everyone' (p. 11), but use your own words. Remember your writing skills.*

Hi,

You'll never guess where I am!

[1] remind [rɪˈmaɪnd] *erinnern* [2] sightseeing [ˈsaɪtsiːɪŋ] *Besichtigung von Sehenswürdigkeiten*

***b)*** *Write a summary of the following story in about 150 words in your exercise book.*

## A birthday surprise

It would be Nina's birthday soon. Her brother David and some friends had planned a birthday surprise for her – a trip to Kakadu National Park.

The group left early on their drive. They laughed, joked and talked about what they might do there: walking, rock climbing, fishing, swimming, picknicking by the river.

'You must be joking! What about the crocs?' said David, who was always careful and never did anything dangerous.

Cathy said that most of the crocs in Kakadu were freshwater crocs, smaller and not aggressive like 'salties'.

Mike argued that thousands of visitors went to Kakadu, but only two or three died each year in a croc attack. But Mike loved an adventure. He loved scary things too.

'I agree,' said Nina, who had always been the wild one in the family. 'The park rangers take visitor safety seriously. They even check for crocs by helicopter. David, don't spoil[1] our fun! You're always scared of something. Relax! I always say: No risk, no fun!'

'So they've closed Twin Falls for swimming for no reason, have they? Why do you think there are crocodile warning signs everywhere? Not even the rangers can give you a guarantee that there will be no salties in the area. There are no guarantees,' David continued[2] in a serious voice.

'Come on, guys, no more arguing. It's Nina's birthday tomorrow, and we're going to have a great time, eh, Nina?' said Mike laughing.

In the evening they celebrated[3] Nina's birthday round a campfire at the campsite. Nina was really happy.

The next day they went to the famous Jim Jim Falls. Nina wanted to see the beautiful natural pools. It was hot and Mike wanted to swim in the cool, clear water. The way there was a difficult climb over rocks. Mike and Nina loved rock climbing, so they soon left the others behind.

Suddenly David noticed that the two had disappeared. Nervously he shouted their names, but they were nowhere. 'This is crazy,' said David. 'We said we would all stay together.' Just then David fell and hurt his foot.

Cathy tried to calm him down, but she was worried too. 'We'll just wait here. You can't climb anyway, if your foot hurts.' But after two hours Mike and Nina still hadn't returned[4]. David felt sick with fear. The minutes seemed like hours. The waiting went on ...

'Hey, you lazy guys! Where were you? It was great up at the pool!' shouted Mike's voice at last. They were back. David threw his arms round his sister. Nina didn't say much ...

Back home after the trip, Nina said to David, 'I have to tell you about what happened up at the falls. A huge saltie suddenly appeared at the edge[5] of the pool only ten metres away. I was terrified, Mike too – but he would never tell you. I couldn't move at first, but the croc came closer, so fast. We just dropped our stuff and ran away over the rocks – lucky that salties are bad climbers. We were too scared to go back, so we had to wait until it had gone – the worst two hours of my life. We could both have been eaten alive if we had jumped in the water. I'm so sorry about what I said about you – you know. You were right – there are no guarantees. And David, please don't tell Mum and Dad ...'

[1] spoil [spɔɪl] *verderben* [2] continue [kən'tɪnju:] *fortsetzen, andauern* [3] celebrate ['selɪbreɪt] *feiern* [4] return [rɪ'tɜ:n] *zurückkehren* [5] edge [edʒ] *Rand, Ufer*

SPEAKING

## 5 SPEAKING Travelling 7

*a) At a travel agency in Australia you want to ask about tours to Uluru for you and your family. Listen (7) and speak to the assistant: ask questions or form sentences in the pauses.*

*Assistant* G'day! How can I help you?
*You* ...

1 Grüße ebenfalls und frage, was man bei der Uluru-Tour alles sehen kann.
2 Frage, wann die Tour losgeht.
3 Frage, wie lange die Tour dauert.
4 Frage, ob man auf der Tour Frühstück bekommt.
5 Frage, wie viel die Tour kostet und was im Preis inbegriffen ist.
6 Sage, du möchtest die Tour für zwei Erwachsene und zwei Schüler für morgen buchen.

*b) Describe picture A or B: the background, the colours, the atmosphere. Say what the people in the picture are doing and how you think they feel. Talk for about two minutes. You can record what you say.*

*I'd like to talk about picture A ...*

MEDIATION

## 6 MEDIATION Berlin tours

*An Australian student would like to go to Berlin for a weekend and he asks you what you can see there. You find a brochure about Berlin tours. Write down the most important things for him in English in your exercise book.*

**Entdecken Sie Berlin mit Alpha Tours – wann und wie Sie wollen**

Genießen Sie eine geführte Tour mit dem Bus, Fahrrad oder zu Fuß zu den vielen Sehenswürdigkeiten der Hauptstadt. Wir organisieren Touren jeder Art für große und mittlere Reisegruppen sowie für kleine Gruppen von 8 bis 12 Personen – und das jeden Tag! Wählen Sie Ihre spezielle Tour aus unseren vielen Angeboten aus!
Entdecken Sie u.a. folgende Highlights:
Regierungsviertel, Berliner Reichstag, Brandenburger Tor, Checkpoint Charlie, Mauerreste, Museumsinsel, Fernsehturm, Kaiser-Wilhelm-Gedächtniskirche, DDR Museum, Berliner Dom, Potsdamer Platz, Schloss Charlottenburg.

Wir bieten:
- moderne klimatisierte Reisebusse, neue bequeme Stadträder.
- Vormittags-, Nachmittags- und Abendtouren mit sämtlichen Eintrittsgeldern inklusive.
- genug Zeit für Fotostops und Erfrischungspausen bei allen Touren.
- bei Ganztagstouren ist auch ein Mittagessen enthalten.
- erfahrene Stadtführer/innen, die mehrere Fremdsprachen sprechen.

Besuchen Sie unsere Website, um Tourbeschreibungen, Preisinformationen, Adressen unserer Filialen und vieles mehr in Erfahrung zu bringen. Rufen Sie uns an oder kommen Sie ganz einfach vorbei!
Tel.: 030-529 487–0 / www.alphatoursberlin.com

## How did you do?

*Check your answers to the exercises on p. 79. Then answer the questions below with Yes or No. If you tick No or would like some extra practice on that point, go to the exercise in your workbook (▸ pp. 50–70).*

### 1 LISTENING Summer vacation

| | Yes | No | Exercise |
|---|---|---|---|
| 1 Hast du dir vor dem 1. Hören die Fragen gründlich durchgelesen? | ☐ | ☐ | ▸ 1, 2 |
| 2 Hast du die Detailfragen ohne Probleme beantworten können? | ☐ | ☐ | ▸ 3, 4 |

### 2 LISTENING A day in the life of…

| | Yes | No | Exercise |
|---|---|---|---|
| 1 Konntest du nach dem 1. Hören beurteilen, um welche Themen es im Interview geht? | ☐ | ☐ | ▸ 1, 2 |
| 2 Hast du dir beim 1. Hören Notizen gemacht (Zahlen, Daten, Namen)? | ☐ | ☐ | ▸ 3, 5 |
| 3 Konntest du den australischen Akzent mühelos verstehen? | ☐ | ☐ | ▸ 7 |
| 4 Konntest du dem Sprechtempo mühelos folgen? | ☐ | ☐ | ▸ 8 |

### 3 READING Sydney for everyone

| | Yes | No | Exercise |
|---|---|---|---|
| 1 Konntest du schnell herausfinden, um was es in dem Text geht? | ☐ | ☐ | ▸ 10, 16a |
| 2 Hast du nach Schlüsselwörtern (*key words*) gesucht, um Antworten zu finden? | ☐ | ☐ | ▸ 11, 12 |
| 3 Konntest du die Antworten auf Detailfragen problemlos finden? | ☐ | ☐ | ▸ 13, 14, 16 |
| 4 Hast du die Bedeutung unbekannter Wörter erschließen können? | ☐ | ☐ | ▸ 15, 16b |

### 4 a) WRITING An e-mail

| | Yes | No | Exercise |
|---|---|---|---|
| 1 Hast du deine Ideen mithilfe eines *brainstorming* gesammelt und dazu Notizen gemacht? | ☐ | ☐ | ▸ 17 |
| 2 Hast du einige der 5 *Ws* am Anfang deines Textes berücksichtigt? | ☐ | ☐ | ▸ 18 |
| 3 Hast du Informationen aus Exercise 1 benutzt und mit eigenen Worten beschrieben? | ☐ | ☐ | ▸ 19 |
| 4 Hast du passende Adjektive (z.B. *interesting, old*) für deine Beschreibungen benutzt? | ☐ | ☐ | ▸ 33 |
| 5 Hast du hauptsächlich das *simple past* (z.B. *went, walked*) benutzt? | ☐ | ☐ | ▸ 29 |
| 6 Hast du deine Wortstellung (z.B. in Nebensätzen) überprüft? | ☐ | ☐ | ▸ 34 |
| 7 Hast du *linking words*, z.B. *but, after, before, while, because, although, so* benutzt? | ☐ | ☐ | ▸ 31 |
| 8 Hast du deine Rechtschreibung/Grammatik überprüft und deine Fehler korrigiert? | ☐ | ☐ | ▸ 35 |

### 4 b) WRITING A summary

| | Yes | No | Exercise |
|---|---|---|---|
| 1 Hast du die wichtigsten Ereignisse erkannt und dazu Notizen gemacht? | ☐ | ☐ | ▸ 17 |
| 2 Hast du die 5 *Ws* am Anfang deiner *summary* berücksichtigt? | ☐ | ☐ | ▸ 18 |
| 3 Hast du die wichtigsten Ereignisse mit eigenen Worten wiedergegeben? | ☐ | ☐ | ▸ 19, 30 |
| 4 Hast du den Unterschied zwischen dem *simple present* und *present progressive* beachtet? | ☐ | ☐ | ▸ 28 |
| 5 Hast du deine Wortstellung (z.B. in Nebensätzen) überprüft? | ☐ | ☐ | ▸ 34 |
| 6 Hast du *linking words*, z.B. *but, after, while, because, although, so* benutzt? | ☐ | ☐ | ▸ 31 |
| 7 Hast du deine Rechtschreibung/Grammatik überprüft und deine Fehler korrigiert? | ☐ | ☐ | ▸ 35 |

### 5 a) SPEAKING Travelling

| | Yes | No | Exercise |
|---|---|---|---|
| 1 Hast du problemlos passende Fragen mit *do/does* oder mit Fragewörtern bilden können? | ☐ | ☐ | ▸ 22 |
| 2 Hast du in den Pausen schnell genug die passenden Fragen stellen können? | ☐ | ☐ | ▸ 23b, 24c |
| 3 Hast du die notwendigen Vokabeln gewusst? | ☐ | ☐ | ▸ 23a |

### 5 b) SPEAKING Travelling

| | Yes | No | Exercise |
|---|---|---|---|
| 1 Hast du bei der Bildbeschreibung Ortsangaben (z.B. *on the right/left*) benutzt? | ☐ | ☐ | ▸ 23a |
| 2 Hast du mit dem *present progressive* (z.B. *is sitting*) beschrieben, was die Personen gerade tun? | ☐ | ☐ | ▸ 28 |
| 3 Hast du die Atmosphäre der Bilder mit passenden Adjektiven beschrieben? | ☐ | ☐ | ▸ 33 |
| 4 Hast du wichtige Vokabeln für die Bildbeschreibung gewusst? | ☐ | ☐ | ▸ 23a |

### 6 MEDIATION Berlin tours

| | Yes | No | Exercise |
|---|---|---|---|
| 1 Hast du beachtet, mit eigenen Worten nur das Wesentliche weiterzugeben bzw. nicht alles wörtlich zu übersetzen? | ☐ | ☐ | ▸ 25 |
| 2 Hast du (falls nötig) für unbekannte Wörter Umschreibungen benutzt (*paraphrasing*)? | ☐ | ☐ | ▸ 32 |

# Unit 2 The world of work

## 1 WORDS Jobs ▸ pp. 32–33

*a) Collect the names of jobs on pp. 32–33 of your student's book. Write a list.*

theme park worker, ______________________________

______________________________

*b) Complete the sentences with job names from a).*

1 

I know quite a lot about cars.
I'd like to be _a mechanic_ .

4 

I enjoy cooking and I'd like to have my own restaurant one day. But first
I'd like to be ______________ in a big hotel kitchen.

2 

I'm quite artistic.
I'd like to work in a theatre as
______________ .

5 

I like looking after children. I'd like
to be ______________
at a kindergarten.

3 

I like talking to customers and answering their questions. I'd like
to be ______________
in a bank maybe.

1601
1602

6 

I'm a sporty person and I'm interested in health and fitness.
Maybe I'd make a good ______________
______________ .

*c) Make three lists in your exercise book. Write two more jobs for each list.*

| Jobs inside | Jobs outside | Jobs inside and outside |
| --- | --- | --- |
| customer adviser, | gardener, | police officer, |

## 2 Blue box: ask/tell/expect/want sb. to do sth. ▸ p. 34, p. 177

*Luke doesn't really know what kind of job he wants to do. What do other people want him to do?*

| | |
| --- | --- |
| 1 *Dad* | 'Why not train as a car mechanic? That's a great job.' |
| 2 *Mum* | 'Work hard and get your GCSEs first.' |
| 3 *Brother* | 'Start an apprenticeship at a bank.' |
| 4 *Girlfriend* | 'Do a computer course. You're good with computers.' |
| 5 *Careers teacher* | 'Have a chat with me on Tuesday next week.' |

*Complete Luke's sentences with object + to-infinitive.*

1 Dad wants _me to train as a car mechanic._

2 Mum expects ______________________________

3 My brother told ______________________________

1603

4 My girlfriend wants ______________________________

5 Mr Ray, our careers teacher, asked ______________________________

## 3 WORDS Personal qualities ▸ p. 36

*Find words that match the jobs and write sentences.*

artistic • calm • careful • clever • confident • energetic • fit • friendly • good at … • hard-working • honest • kind • likeable • logical • organized • polite • punctual • reliable • sporty

1 I think a builder has to be *fit, reliable and hard-working.*

2 I think a fitness instructor ___

3 I think a customer adviser ___

4 I think an office worker ___

5 I think a nurse ___

6 I think a police officer ___

## 4 WORDS What kind of person are you? ▸ p. 36

**a)** *Imagine that you are having an interview for a job that you would really like to do. The interviewer says: 'Tell me about yourself. Why do you want to work for us?' How would you answer these questions? First say which job you want, then make notes. You can use the phrases below and the words in exercise 3. Write your answer in a few sentences in your exercise book.*

I'd like a job as … • I'm quite … and I'm very interested in … • I think I'd be right for this job because …

**b)** *How do you think these people would describe you? Complete the sentences. You can use the words and phrases in the blue and yellow boxes below and the green box in exercise 3.*

a bit • quite • very • (not) always • sometimes • usually

boring • funny • interested in … • likeable • nervous • noisy • quiet • relaxed • serious • tidy

1 My friends would describe me as ___

2 I think my family ___

3 Maybe my teachers ___

1704

**c)** *How do interviewers like their future apprentices to be? What do you think are the 'top ten' most important qualities? Write your ideas in your exercise book.*

*I think it´s important to be …  It´s also an advantage if you´re …  You should also show that you´re …*

## 5 REVISION After school (Gerund as subject and object) ▸ p. 36

*Complete the sentences with your own ideas. Use gerunds, for example* I enjoy working in a café *or* Working in an office is something I've never wanted to do.

1 When I leave school, I'll really enjoy ______

2 ______ is something I've always wanted to do.

3 ______ is very important for kids our age.

4 I can't really imagine ______

5 I don't mind ______

1805 6 I prefer[1] ______ to ______, so that will be important when I apply for a job.

### Now you

*Think about these questions: What are you good at? What do you like doing? What are you used to doing? What are you not interested in? What do you hate doing? Write at least one sentence each in your exercise book.*

## 6 EVERYDAY ENGLISH MEDIATION Part-time jobs ▸ p. 37 • WB (p. 76)

Test

*You want to tell your friend about two part-time jobs in the UK. Tell him/her in German about a) what you have to do in the jobs below and b) what kind of people they need. First make notes.*

**1 High Street Café**

We need a **part-time waiter/waitress** for our busy café. You will help in the kitchen, clean and lay tables, serve drinks, cakes, snacks and ice cream from 2 to 6 pm, Saturday and Sunday.
You should work quickly, be friendly, polite, tidy and good at Maths.
Pay above average.
Phone us on 01288 361255 for more information.

______

**2 Are you a dog lover?**

We walk dogs for owners who are ill or don't have time to give their dogs long walks.
We are looking for young people who like dogs and like walking. You will pick up the dog from its home and take it back.
Hours: 7 am to 1 pm or 1 pm to 7 pm in every kind of weather.
A bike to get you from walk to walk would be an advantage.
Write to: dogwalkers@blue.com

______

WB, pp. 65–66

[1] prefer [prɪˈfɜː] *vorziehen*

## 7 EVERYDAY ENGLISH WRITING A job application form ► p. 37

*a) Read about John.*

John Miller is 15. He lives with his family and their dog at 7 Castle Road, Selby YO8 4TW.

His home telephone number is 01757 809995. He hasn't got a mobile phone at the moment, but you can write to him at j.miller@afl.com. His hobbies are computers, reading, football and cycling. He knows a lot about bikes and often wins local cycle races.

He's been at Kingsway High School since 2005. He has GCSEs in English, Maths, German, Science and Geography. In July and August 2009 he worked at Samuel Sports. He sold customers sports shoes and equipment. Now he's looking for a holiday job for this summer. He's friendly, helpful and good with customers. He would like to work at Wilson Cycles, a big new bike shop in town.

*b) Fill in John's application form for Wilson Cycles with the correct information from a).*

Job application form for WILSON CYCLES

**PERSONAL DETAILS**

First name(s) ____________ Surname ____________

Address ____________

Tel no (home) ____________ Tel no (mobile phone) ____________

E-mail address ____________

**WORK EXPERIENCE**

| Company | From | To | Job details |
|---|---|---|---|
| | | | |
| | | | |

**EDUCATION**

| School | From | To | School subjects |
|---|---|---|---|
| | | | |
| | | | |

**HOBBIES AND INTERESTS**

____________

*c) Why does John have a good chance of getting the job? Write a few sentences.*

*I think John has a good chance because* ____________

____________

____________

## 8 STUDY SKILLS An English CV

▸ p. 39 • SF (p. 152)

*a) Which information should be on your English CV? Tick the correct boxes.*

| | | | | | |
|---|---|---|---|---|---|
| home address | ✔ | hobbies and interests | ☐ | telephone number | ☐ |
| first name and surname | ☐ | nationality | ☐ | date of birth | ☐ |
| education | ☐ | e-mail address | ☐ | references | ☐ |
| qualifications | ☐ | work experience | ☐ | place of birth | ☐ |
| personal statement | ☐ | sex | ☐ | other skills | ☐ |

*b) Put the information that you have ticked in a) in the usual order for your English CV. Check with the CV on p. 38 of your student's book.*

1 *first name and surname* 7 ______
2 ______ 8 ______
3 ______ 9 ______
4 ______ 10 ______
5 ______ 11 ______
6 ______

*c) Use the CV on p. 38 of your student's book to write your own English CV on the computer or in your exercise book.*

**INFO BOX**

In Germany you include a photo with your CV, but not with your English CV for the UK.

## 9 STUDY SKILLS A letter of application

▸ p. 39 • SF (p. 153)

*a) Complete the information about formal letters.*

1 If you start a formal letter with 'Dear Sir/Madam', you usually end it with ______ .

2 If you know the name of the person, you start with ______ and end with ______ .

*b) Put the sentences in a logical order and write John's letter of application to Ms Roberts at Wilson Cycles in your exercise book. First, write 2–8 after the sentences. More than one answer is possible.*

Dear Ms Roberts

| | |
|---|---|
| In the last summer holidays I worked (six weeks) at Samuel Sports in George Street. | ☐ |
| I enclose my CV. | ☐ |
| I read your advertisement in the Selby Post and would like to apply for a job as assistant sales person. | *1* |
| I look forward to hearing from you soon. | ☐ |
| I am very interested in cycles and have won local cycle races. | ☐ |
| I enjoy serving customers and am happy to work in the evenings and on Saturdays. | ☐ |
| The manager at Samuel Sports will be happy to give me a reference. | ☐ |
| Yours sincerely | ☐ |

## 10 SPEAKING COURSE Part 2: Tom's interview (Taking part in a job interview)

▸ p. 41 • WB (p. 73) 🎧 8

**a)** *Tom Wood is preparing for an interview for a summer job at a garden centre. Tick the statements and the questions which he could use at the interview.*

1 Can you tell me what I would have to do exactly? ✔
2 Who can I contact if I have a question? ☐
3 Would I have to make the tea? ☐
4 I enjoy working in the garden. I look after my grandmother's garden. She has lots of trees and plants. ☐
5 Well, I think I would really like the work and I'd be good at it. ☐
6 Is the pay good? ☐
7 My last job was awful. The manager wasn't fair. ☐
8 I worked in a busy office last summer. I learned a lot. But I like working outside more. ☐
9 Sorry I'm late. I didn't get the bus because my mum forgot to wake me up. ☐
10 What are the hours of work? ☐
11 I'm careful and reliable. I learn quickly and I work hard when I'm interested in something. ☐

**b)** *Imagine that you are Tom. Listen to the interviewer on your CD (🎧 8) and answer her questions. Read the sentences that you have ticked in a) again before you start. Do the exercise at least twice.*

WB, pp. 63–64

2110

*Interviewer* Good morning. I'm Jane Ashton, the manager. You're Thomas Wood, is that right? Thank you for your application. Did you find us easily?
*You* *Yes, thanks. It was no problem.*
*Interviewer* Now, why did you apply for a gardening job?
*You* ...

## 11 REVISION After the interview (Indirect speech)

▸ p. 42 • WB (p. 76)

*What did Tom tell the interviewer? Complete the sentences. Remember to change the tense.*

1 I'm careful, reliable and hard-working.
2 I like working outside.
3 I have some work experience.
4 I look after my grandmother's garden.
5 I enjoy looking after plants and trees.
6 I can work at weekends.
7 I don't mind working alone.

1 At the interview Tom said that he *was* careful, reliable and hard-working.
2 He told the interviewer that he ____________ working outside.
3 He also said that he ____________ some work experience.
4 He told her that he ____________ after his grandmother's garden.
5 He said that he ____________ looking after plants and trees.
6 He told Ms Ashton that he ____________ work at weekends too.
2111
7 He also said that he ____________ mind working alone.

## 12 Interview tips (Indirect speech: commands and requests) ► p. 42 • WB (p. 77)

*a) Before John Miller went for his interview, he met his friend Jamal, who gave him a few good tips.*

'I've had a few interviews and I've always said something wrong or done something silly because I was too nervous. So I'll give you a few tips.
(1) *Be punctual* and (2) *don't forget* to turn off your phone. My phone once rang in the middle of an interview. I felt awful. (3) Don't show that you're nervous and (4) ask some clever questions. The interviewer will be impressed. (5) It's important to look the interviewer in the eye and (6) don't talk too much. I usually do that! (7) Can you phone me later to give me the news? (8) And if you get the job, can you lend me some money till next month?'

*b) Now complete the text.*

(1) Jamal told John *to be punctual* and (2) *not to* forget to turn off his phone.

(3) He also ______ that he was nervous and (4) told ______ some clever questions. (5) Then he ______ the interviewer in the eye and

(6) ______ too much. (7) Before John left, Jamal ______

2212 (8) Then Jamal ______ till next month – if he got the job.

### Now you

*Think of four more tips that you would give a friend before an interview. Write them in your exercise book.*

*I would tell him/her to ... / I would tell him/her not to ...*

## 13 At the interview (Indirect speech: questions with question words) ► p. 43 • WB (p. 77)

*Ms Roberts asked John these questions at the interview.*

1 Why do you want to work for us?
2 What do you know about Wilson Cycles?
3 What are your strengths?
4 How good are you with customers?
5 What makes one bike more expensive than another?
6 When can you start if we offer you the job?

*Later at home, John told his mum what the interviewer had asked. What did John say?*

1 The interviewer asked me *why I wanted to work for them.*

2 She asked me ______

3 She asked me ______

4 Then she asked ______

5 She wanted to know ______

2213 6 She also wanted to know ______

## 14 What did John ask? (Indirect speech: yes/no questions)

▸ p. 43 • WB (p. 77)

*Jamal wanted to know what questions John had asked at the interview. These were some of his questions.*

1 'Will there be any training first?'
2 'Do you sell very expensive racing bikes?'
3 'Do I have to learn all the technical details?'
4 'Is there a repair service at the centre?'
5 'Can I repair my own bike in my free time?'
6 'Will I be allowed to try out the new bikes?'

1 I asked if there would be any training first.

2 I asked ______

3 I asked ______

4 I wanted to know ______

5 I asked ______

2314 6 I asked ______

## 15 WORDS Getting a job

▸ p. 43

apply • apprenticeship • candidate • confident • CV • decisions • details • education • enclose • experience • fill in • future • pay • polite • qualifications • skills • training

**a)** *Complete the text with words from the box.*

Before you leave school there are some important decisions to make, but whatever job you do in the ______, you'll need some ______. Maybe you'd like to do an ______ for two or three years. The ______ won't be good, but you'll get special job ______ and you'll learn some useful ______. When you ______ for a job, you usually have to ______ an application form which asks for your personal ______, your school ______ and your work ______. You should also ______ your ______ and a formal letter of application. If you are an interesting ______, the company might invite you to an interview. You should be well prepared, friendly and ______ and be ______ about what you are good at. Good luck!

**b)** *Complete the sentences with a word from the same family as the word in brackets ( ).*

1 John read an advertisement (advertise) for a summer job at Wilson Cycles.

2 He sent an ______ (apply) to Ms Roberts, who invited him to an interview.

3 John is a very ______ (energy) person and he has a lot of ______ (strong).

4 For the interview he dressed ______ (suitable) and showed that he was ______ (organize).

2315 5 He hopes Ms Roberts was ______ (impress).

## 16 ENGLISH FOR JOBS LISTENING Phone calls

▸ p. 43 • WB (p. 71) 9

Test

*Mrs Holby is a hard-working manager. Ben, her assistant, writes the times of her appointments and interviews in an appointments diary. Listen to the telephone calls and write the necessary changes in the diary.*

| Monday | Tuesday | Wednesday | Thursday | Friday |
|---|---|---|---|---|
| ~~10.30 Interview Ms Jane Morton~~ | 10.15 Mr D. Thomas, (Bell Electronics) | 8.30 Dentist's appointment | 9.30 Presentation | 8.30 |
| | | 11.00 Interview Ms Maria Langton | | |
| | 2.30 Interview Mr Peter Marlow | | 2.30 Visit to MPR Software, Harrow | 2.00 Interview Mr S. Rogers |

WB, pp. 50–53

## 17 READING WORKING WITH THE TEXT
### How to be a teenage millionaire

▸ pp. 44–46 • WB (pp. 71–72)

**a)** *Put the events of the story on pp. 44–45 in your student's book in the correct order. Write the numbers 2–8 in the boxes.*

- She bought the address whateverlife.com with the money. ☐
- Ashley started to design websites when she was nine years old. 1
- She received her first big cheque. ☐
- She asked her mother for $8. ☐
- Big companies became interested in advertising on her website. ☐
- She's thinking of studying in her dream city, New York. ☐
- She left school just before her 16th birthday. ☐
- She started paying friends to work for her in their free time. ☐

**b)** *How would you describe Ashley? What do you know about her? Tick the correct answers.*

1 She's determined and ambitious. ☐
2 She earns money by selling her designs. ☐
3 She doesn't miss school. ☐
4 She's very successful. ☐
5 She pays people who work for her. ☐
6 She's artistic and hard-working. ☐
7 She lives the normal life of a teenager. ☐
8 Her business brings in $700 a day. ☐

WB, pp. 54–58

**c)** *If Ashley was in your school class, how would you and your classmates feel about it? Would you want to work for her? How would you feel about her strict rules? Explain your arguments. Write in your exercise book.*

2418 *I think it would be fun to have a teenage millionaire as a classmate. First, ...*
2419 *I don't think it would be good to work for somebody in your own school class. First, ...*

## How well can you do these things?

| | Very well | OK | Practise! |
|---|---|---|---|
| **LISTENING AND READING SKILLS:** I can ... | | | |
| ... understand longer conversations and stories even if I don't know some words, e.g. *In the outback* (SB pp. 20–23). | ☐ | ☐ | ☐ |
| ... understand and find detailed information from what I hear or read, e.g. details about Ashley Qualls' business (SB pp. 44–45). | ☐ | ☐ | ☐ |
| ... understand the Australian accent without difficulty, e.g. Rob talking about sports (SB p. 13). | ☐ | ☐ | ☐ |
| **SPEAKING AND WRITING SKILLS:** I can ... | | | |
| ... start and continue a conversation on an everyday topic with someone I don't know. | ☐ | ☐ | ☐ |
| ... describe my personal qualities and my interests at a job interview. | ☐ | ☐ | ☐ |
| ... write a short film review. | ☐ | ☐ | ☐ |
| ... write my CV with the correct format. | ☐ | ☐ | ☐ |
| ... fill in a job application form. | ☐ | ☐ | ☐ |
| ... write a formal letter of application and a formal letter asking for information in a suitable style and format. | ☐ | ☐ | ☐ |
| **MEDIATION SKILLS:** I can ... | | | |
| ... report the most important facts from conversations or written texts, both from German into English and from English into German, e.g. I can talk about English job adverts in German. | ☐ | ☐ | ☐ |
| ... use synonyms or paraphrasing for words and phrases I don't know. | ☐ | ☐ | ☐ |
| **TOPICS:** I have learned ... | | | |
| ... about Australia's geography, history, animals, natural sights (e.g. the outback, Uluru, the Great Barrier Reef) and the School of the Air. | ☐ | ☐ | ☐ |
| ... about Aboriginal culture and history, e.g. the 'Dreamtime' and 'the stolen generations'. | ☐ | ☐ | ☐ |
| ... how to talk about jobs, job applications, work experience and the qualities needed for different jobs. | ☐ | ☐ | ☐ |
| ... how to call about an interview and ask questions about a job. | ☐ | ☐ | ☐ |
| ... how to present myself at an interview. | ☐ | ☐ | ☐ |
| **STUDY AND LANGUAGE SKILLS:** I know ... | | | |
| ... how to understand, talk about and compare bar charts and pie charts. | ☐ | ☐ | ☐ |

**WAYS TO IMPROVE MY ENGLISH SKILLS:** I could ...
(e.g. work through Skills Check 1 again, watch DVDs in English, ...)

_______________________________________________

_______________________________________________

[1] Self-evaluation [ˌself ɪˌvælju'eɪʃn] *Selbsteinschätzung*

# Skills Check 2



## 1 LISTENING First day at work 10

*You are going to hear Jenna talking about her first summer vacation job. First read the sentences, then listen and tick A, B or C. You will hear the recording twice.*

1 Jenna got her first summer vacation job in a ...

- A clothes store.
- B shoe store.
- C designer jeans boutique.

2 She wanted to work there because ...

- A she loves shoes.
- B she couldn't get any other job.
- C the store sold shoes for teenagers.

3 Jenna got the job there because ...

- A she had work experience.
- B they needed someone quickly.
- C she was the only applicant.

4 The first customer bought shoes in ...

- A brown and black.
- B black and blue.
- C blue and brown.

5 The customer paid ... for two pairs of shoes.

- A 155 dollars
- B 310 dollars
- C 410 dollars

6 Jenna didn't know the correct price because ...

- A someone told her the wrong price.
- B there was no price on the shoes.
- C the price on the box was wrong.

7 When Jenna couldn't find the shoes for the second customer, she ...

- A asked the manager.
- B showed the customer different shoes.
- C waited in the store room[1] until the customer had gone.

8 Jenna thought it would be unprofessional to ...

- A say she couldn't find the shoes the customer wanted.
- B ask how the system in the store room worked.
- C hide in the store room.



## 2 READING Jobs

**a)** *Look at the five texts quickly. What are they about? Tick the correct box.*

Young people describing a job they would like to do ☐
Young people describing work experience ☐
Young people describing jobs that they do ☐

**b)** *Read what five young people say. Look at the pictures on the next page. Which picture matches which description? Write A–F in the boxes. There is one picture more than you need.*

1 ☐ I love my job, though it isn't easy. You have to work really hard and the pay isn't good. We work shifts. I often have the night shift, which is quite hard because you're mostly alone, so it's difficult if there's an emergency[2]. I always hope nothing will happen when I'm doing a night shift. We have to know a lot. It's a very responsible job and we mustn't make mistakes. We have to be exact in our work, punctual, reliable, caring and always friendly to our patients.

2 ☐ I work outside half of the time. I don't mind because there's usually something going on. And we work in twos on the street, so there's always a partner to talk to. We are often called to traffic accidents, fights or robberies in the area. I prefer that part of the job to sitting in the office writing up reports, but we have to do that too. There's some routine, but my job is much better than a nine-to-five job, and it's surprising how much crime there is in a small town. We're always busy. It's never boring.

[1] store room *Lager* [2] emergency [ɪ'mɜːdʒənsi] *Notfall*

3 ☐ In my job you have to be calm and organized and you have to be good in a team. I work with my boss and his partner. I always have to be punctual and reliable, but that's no problem. I had to learn a lot and do exams and I'm still training, so I don't do operations myself yet. I'm glad that we can help old ladies and children when their pets are ill. But we also help farm animals, cows, sheep and horses. You shouldn't mind getting your hands dirty. It's a good feeling being able to help and save lives.

4 ☐ I'm an outdoor person. I definitely couldn't work in an office all day sitting at a desk and looking at a computer. I work for a company in town, but we have projects all over the area. Sometimes they're really big projects, office blocks or industrial parks. My job isn't very nice in winter when it's cold and it rains a lot. You have to be fit and quite strong. We carry[1] building materials and we start early. It's nice to look at a beautiful new building and know that you were part of it.

5 ☐ This is my second year as a trainee[2]. It's hard work and I had to start from the bottom, cleaning floors and plates – pretty boring. At first I learned all the standard dishes, but I really enjoy being artistic with food and cooking my own dishes. I hope to have my own restaurant one day.

A

Lucy

B
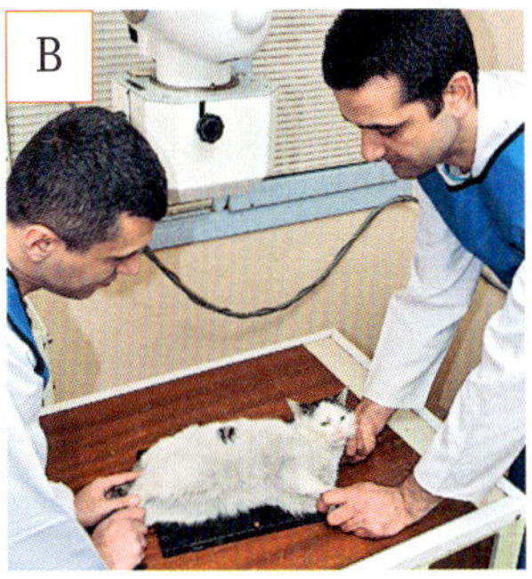
Adam

C

Penny

D
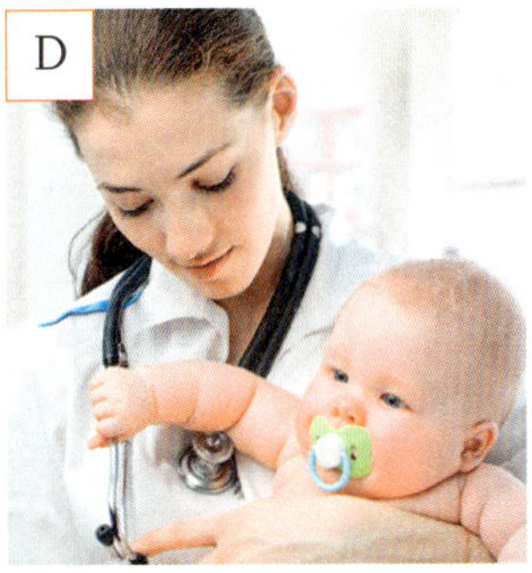
Lauren

E

Nick

F

Sam

c) *Write the correct name.*

1 Who would like to own his own business? ____________

2 Who likes being part of a big project? ____________

3 Who doesn't like working night shifts? ____________

4 Who works outdoors about 50% ? ____________

5 Who has completed one year of training? ____________

6 Who assists at operations? ____________

7 Who hates office work? ____________

8 Who has to be fit? ____________

[1] carry [ˈkæri] *tragen* [2] trainee [ˌtreɪˈniː] *Auszubildende/r*

## 3 WRITING A formal letter

*You would like to apply for this summer job in London. Write a formal letter of application to the company. Think about the form and about how to start and end your letter. Write 80–100 words.*

**Ferienjob in London?**

Wir suchen deutschsprachige Aushilfen für unseren Touristendienst in London (mehrere Stellen) für jeweils 6 bis 8 Wochen in der Zeit von Mai bis September.
Senden Sie bitte Ihre englischsprachigen Bewerbungsunterlagen an:
London Tourist Service
15 Regent Street
London SW1
England

LONDON Tourist Service

## 4 WRITING Your CV

*Now write your CV to send with your application. Which information do you need (personal details, education, qualifications) and in which order? Don't forget a short personal statement.*



## 5 WRITING An informal letter

*Write an informal letter to an English friend in London telling him/her about the job in the advert. Say why the job interests you and write about the good and bad things. Brainstorm your ideas first (mind map, list). Write about 100 words in your exercise book.*

## 6 SPEAKING Jobs and work experience

*a) Look at the two pictures and describe the jobs. Compare their advantages and disadvantages. What are the people doing? How do you think the people feel when they're doing these jobs? Which job would you like? Why? Make notes in English in your exercise book and talk for about two minutes. You can record what you say.*

1

2

*b) Prepare answers to these questions and talk for about two minutes. You can record what you say.*

- Why do you think work experience is important for young people?
- Tell me about your two weeks of work experience.
- What did you like about it and what didn't you like?
- Do you have a weekend job or an after-school job?
- What kind of job would you like to do when you leave school?



## 7 MEDIATION Small ads

*You have met an American student. She doesn't speak much German but would like to have a job for a few hours a day. You find some suitable jobs in the local newspaper. Make notes in English in your exercise book first. Then tell her about the jobs.*

1 **Café am Brunnen**

**Aushilfe** gesucht f. ca. 3 Stunden vorm. od. nachm. Arbeiten in Küche und Café (z.B. Gemüse putzen, Küche aufräumen, Tische decken u. abräumen). Servieren von Eis und Kuchen im Gastgarten.
Gute Bezahlung.
Tel.: 793 501

2 **Hotel am Domplatz**

Für die Rezeption suchen wir **ab sofort** eine Kraft mit sehr guten **Englischkenntnissen.**
Aufgaben: telefonische Auskunft u. Betreuung ausländischer Gäste.
Erfahrung in der Hotelbranche erwünscht, aber nicht Voraussetzung. Halbtags od. stundenweise als Aushilfe.
**Überdurchschnittliche Bezahlung.**
Tel.: 482 502 (Fr. Lenz)

3 **Englischsprachige Kinderbetreuung**

für amerikanische Familie gesucht (Kinder 2 und 4 J.).
Mo–Fr, 13–17 Uhr. Keine Arbeit im Haushalt.
Führerschein nicht erforderlich.
Tel.: 602 335

4 Student/in für **englische Konversation** gesucht.
Mo u. Do vorm. je 2 St. (Gruppe 6 Pers.),
2. Gruppe Di u. Fr möglich, **native speaker** willkommen! Deutschkenntnisse nicht erforderlich. Tel.: 496 395 (Vera)

*Well, there's a job in a café. You have to ...*

## How did you do?

*Check your answers to the exercises on p. 80. Then answer the questions below with Yes or No. If you tick No or would like some extra practice on that point, go to the exercise in your workbook (▸ pp. 50–70).*

| | Yes | No | Exercise |
|---|---|---|---|
| **1 LISTENING First day at work** | | | |
| 1 Konntest du nach dem 1. Hören beurteilen, um was es im Wesentlichen geht? | ☐ | ☐ ▸ | 1, 2, 9a |
| 2 Hast du dir beim 1. Hören Angaben zu Zahlen und andere Details notiert? | ☐ | ☐ ▸ | 3, 5 |
| 3 Konntest du den amerikanischen Akzent erkennen und mühelos verstehen? | ☐ | ☐ ▸ | 6, 7, 9 |
| 4 Konntest du dem Sprechtempo problemlos folgen? | ☐ | ☐ ▸ | 8, 9 |
| **2 READING Jobs** | | | |
| 1 Konntest du schnell herausfinden, um was es jeweils in den Texten geht? | ☐ | ☐ | 10, 16a |
| 2 Konntest du Antworten auf Detailfragen problemlos finden? | ☐ | ☐ ▸ | 13, 14, 16 |
| 3 Hast du die Bedeutung unbekannter Wörter erschließen können? | ☐ | ☐ ▸ | 15, 16b |
| **3 WRITING A formal letter** | | | |
| 1 Hast du genau gewusst, wie die äußere Form eines *formal letter* aussieht? | ☐ | ☐ ▸ | 20b |
| 2 Hast du eine höfliche Anrede und passende Schlussformel benutzt? | ☐ | ☐ ▸ | 20a |
| 3 Hast du deine Rechtschreibung/Grammatik überprüft und deine Fehler korrigiert? | ☐ | ☐ ▸ | 35 |
| **4 WRITING Your CV** | | | |
| 1 Hast du alle erforderlichen Informationen in der richtigen Reihenfolge präsentiert? | ☐ | ☐ ▸ | 21a+c |
| 2 Ist es dir leicht gefallen, ein kurzes, treffendes *personal statement* zu schreiben? | ☐ | ☐ ▸ | 21b |
| **5 WRITING An informal letter** | | | |
| 1 Hast du eine passende Gruß- und Schlussformel benutzt? | ☐ | ☐ ▸ | 17b |
| 2 Hast du deinem Text eine Struktur gegeben und zuvor Ideen gesammelt und Notizen gemacht? | ☐ | ☐ ▸ | 17a |
| **6 SPEAKING Jobs and work experience** | | | |
| 1 Hast du mit dem *present progressive* (z.B. *is sitting*) beschrieben, was die Personen auf den Bildern gerade tun? | ☐ | ☐ ▸ | 28 |
| 2 Hast du die Jobs mit passenden Adjektiven (z.B. *bored, good*) beschrieben? | ☐ | ☐ ▸ | 33 |
| 3 Hast du wichtige Vokabeln für die Bildbeschreibung (z.B. *in the background* usw.) gewusst? | ☐ | ☐ ▸ | 23a |
| 4 Hast du problemlos deine Meinung zu den Fragen ausdrücken können? | ☐ | ☐ ▸ | 23b |
| 5 Hast du über deine *work experience* im *simple past* (z.B. *worked*) erzählt? | ☐ | ☐ ▸ | 29 |
| **7 MEDIATION Small ads** | | | |
| 1 Hast du beachtet, mit eigenen Worten nur das Wesentliche weiterzugeben bzw. nicht alles wörtlich zu übersetzen? | ☐ | ☐ ▸ | 25, 26 |
| 2 Hast du (falls nötig) für unbekannte Wörter Umschreibungen benutzt (*paraphrasing*)? | ☐ | ☐ ▸ | 32 |
| 3 Hast du modale Hilfsverben richtig benutzt (*can, have to, needn't* usw.)? | ☐ | ☐ ▸ | 27 |

# Unit 3 Teen world

## 1 Keira, Connor and Lina ▸ pp. 48–49

Test

*a) Read p. 48 in your student's book again. Are the statements below true or false? Mark a letter.*

| | True | False |
|---|---|---|
| 1 Lina comes from the UK. | K | E |
| 2 Keira hasn't got any brothers or sisters. | N | E |
| 3 Lina is very interested in fashion. | T | I |
| 4 Connor thinks his parents are strict. | D | N |
| 5 Lina works very hard at school and at home. | L | G |
| 6 Connor would love to have a career in a bank. | E | R |
| 7 Keira enjoys spending money. | A | S |

*b) If your answers are correct, you can spell the name of a country with the letters:*

____________________

*c) Would you like to be friends with Keira, Connor or Lina? Say why. In your exercise book, make notes, then write a paragraph.*

Ideas: *hard-working • fun • serious about … • relaxed • ambitious • determined • interested in … • computer-crazy • good at … • loves … • crazy about … • likes …*

*I think I would like to have … as a friend because …*

## 2 WORDS Blue box: Verbs and their nouns ▸ p. 51, p. 182

*a) Write nouns from the verbs. Eight more nouns have the ending **-tion/-ion**. The others are different.*

1 produce: *production*

2 apply: __________

3 organize: __________

4 decide: __________

5 advertise: __________

6 present: __________

7 translate: __________

8 communicate: __________

9 advise: __________

10 attract: __________

11 apologize: __________

12 revise: __________

*b) Complete the text about Adnan with suitable verbs and their nouns from a).*

Adnan works hard at school and he plays football in his free time, so he has to *organize* his homework well. He's doing a Maths test next week but he hasn't done much __________ yet. He has some French homework too, a __________ from French into English. In Geography he has to give a __________ about Bosnia. Adnan wants to be a top footballer, but his girlfriend thinks he should write some __________ for an apprenticeship. Maybe she's right. But it will be Adnan's own __________ .

3202

## 3 EVERYDAY ENGLISH SPEAKING Teens and their mobiles ▸ p. 52 🎧 11

*Listen to what six British students say about how they use their mobile phones. In the pauses, give your opinion on what each student says. Use:*

WB, pp. 63–64

- *I agree with … (completely).*
- *I don't agree with … (at all).*
- *I can't understand why …*
- *In my opinion, …*
- *I don't think it's fair to …*
- *I think it's a good idea to …*
- *I think … is right/wrong.*
- *I think it's stupid to say …*

3303
3304
*1 Listen to Emma. This is how you might give your opinion:*
I agree with Emma's parents. In my opinion, Emma is unfair. Why should her parents pay so much money just for her fun? I think that a lot of Emma's phone calls and messages are probably unnecessary …

## 4 EVERYDAY ENGLISH WRITING A formal letter ▸ p. 52 • SF (p. 153)

Test

*Write a formal letter to the editor of the Bristol Evening Post about mobiles in schools. Say why you think schools should ban/allow[1] mobiles in classrooms. Give at least two reasons for your opinion. Use your exercise book or computer. Don't forget your name, address and the date. Use a formal beginning and ending.*

…
Dear …
I would like to discuss the question of mobile phones in schools.
I think schools should/should not allow students to have mobiles.
First, …
Second, …
What do other readers think?
…

WB, pp. 59–62

**INFO BOX**

In Germany 92 % of young people aged 12 to 19 have a mobile phone, 69 % of kids from 10 to 13 and 16 % of kids under 10!
Half the kids pay part of their monthly phone bill. 20 % of the kids pay the bill themselves!
(Source: KidsVA 2009, Egmont Ehapa Verlag)

## 5 WORDS Mobile phones ▸ p. 53

***a)*** *Choose words from the box that go with the verbs. Sometimes there's more than one correct word.*

a call • your mailbox • a message • a phone number • a photo • a ringtone • the time

1 check your mailbox, the time, …
2 download ______
3 miss ______
4 save ______
5 make ______
6 take ______
7 text ______
8 receive/get ______

***b)*** *Now complete what Rubina says about how she uses her mobile with words from a).*

I make most calls at the weekend. I text five ______ a day on average and I ______ my mailbox every day. I always ______ phone numbers of new contacts. I don't often ______ photos, but sometimes I ______ a new ringtone. I ______ a few text messages from friends, but I don't always read them till later. If I ______ a call, I usually phone back, but not always. Oh, and I don't need a watch any more. I use my mobile to check ______ or set an alarm. My mobile makes life easier, but I'm never its slave!
3305

[1] allow [əˈlaʊ] *erlauben*

## 6 ENGLISH FOR JOBS Useful job phrases ▸ p. 53

*a) Who says what? Write C (customer) or S (shop assistant).*

Can I help you? S
There's your receipt. ____
I'd like …/I'm looking for … ____
There's your change. ____
Do you want to pay cash or by credit card? ____
This one's a bit more expensive. ____
3406 Have you got this in other colours/sizes? ____

I'll take this/these, please. C
Would you like anything else? ____
That's … euros/pounds, please. ____
I'm just looking, thank you. ____
Just a moment. I'll check. ____
These are very popular. ____
Where's the … department[1], please? ____

*b) Write a dialogue between a shop assistant and a teenager in your exercise book. Decide what the teenager wants to buy, for example a pullover, a pair of jeans, a shirt, etc. Use as many phrases from a) as you can.*

Hello.
Can I help you?

Maybe.
I'm looking for…

## 7 WORDS Shane's ASBO ▸ p. 54

*Choose words from the box in the correct form to complete the sentences.*

ban • behaviour • bullies • cause • court • fights • head teacher • law • motorbikes • offer • order • organization • police • punishment • steal • troublemaker • vandalize

1 The 'B' in 'ASBO' means ____________.
2 The 'O' in 'ASBO' means ____________.
3 Shane was a ____________.
4 He broke the ________ many times.
3407 5 He ________ trouble in his local area and at school.
6 He rode ____________ on the pavement.
7 He ____________ cars and parks.
8 He got into ____________ with other teenagers.
9 He was given a four-year ASBO by the ____________.
10 Was that a fair ____________?

## Now you

*Why do you think some young people become troublemakers? Write your opinion in an e-mail to a teen magazine. Write the text in your exercise book.*

Ideas: *feel bored and angry • see no future without a job or money • don't care • want to have 'fun'*

*Dear mag,*
*I would like to give my opinion on teenage antisocial behaviour …*

[1] department *Abteilung*

## 8 SPEAKING COURSE Part 3: Discussion phrases (Having a discussion)

▸ p. 56 • WB (p. 73) 12, 13

*a) Tick the correct phrase. During a discussion, what would you say …*

1 when you want to know someone's opinion?

A I see what you mean. B What do you think? C Could you say that again, please?

2 when you say what you think?

A I agree with you. B In my opinion, … C No, that's not right.

3 when you think/feel the same as the speaker?

A Could you say that again? B I agree with you. C Let me explain.

4 when you want to say that you understand the speaker's point?

A I see what you mean. B Wait a minute. Let me finish.
C Sorry, I don't agree with you.

5 when you are speaking and someone else starts to speak?

A No, that's not right. B Could you say that again, please?
C Wait a minute. Let me finish.

6 when you don't think/feel the same as the speaker?

A Sorry, I don't agree with you. B I know you're right.
C That's true.

7 when you think what someone said is wrong?

A I don't understand what you mean. B You're right. C No, that's not right.

*b) Read the discussion phrases below. Then listen (12) to Guy, Mel and Ali, three British teenagers who are talking about ASBOs. Write down the order that you hear the discussion phrases in (2–11).*

| | | | |
|---|---|---|---|
| I agree with you. | ( ) | That's a good point. | ( ) |
| In my opinion, … | ( 1 ) | I see what you mean. | ( ) |
| Wait a minute. Let me finish. | ( ) | Sorry, but I don't agree with you. | ( ) |
| What do you think? | ( ) | No, that's not right. | ( ) |
| First, … | ( ) | That's true. | ( ) |
| Second, … | ( ) | | |

*c) Listen again (13) to the discussion and in the pauses fill in the missing phrases from b). Do this exercise at least twice.*

WB, pp. 63–64

3508

## 9 WORDS Adjectives: 'interested' or 'interesting'? ▸ p. 57

*a) Find matching pairs.*

| | | | |
|---|---|---|---|
| interesting | gelangweilt | excited | überrascht |
| bored | interessant | surprised | erstaunt |
| shocking | schockiert | amazing | aufgeregt |
| boring | interessiert | surprising | erstaunlich |
| interested | schockierend | exciting | aufregend |
| shocked | langweilig | amazed | überraschend |

*b) Complete what Rick says with words from a).*

We watched a scary film last night. It was quite exciting (excite) at first. In the middle I got a bit ______ (bore) because the story wasn't really ______ (interest). But the special effects were ______ (amaze). My sister looked quite ______ (shock) because the cybermonsters were so ugly. Of course the end wasn't ______ (surprise). It was stupid really. My sister didn't seem to find the story ______ (bore) at all. Just imagine, after the film was over, she said she was ______ (surprise) that I watched such rubbish! I'm sure she enjoyed the film more than I did!

3609

## 10 Extra Kids getting into trouble (Understanding participle clauses) ▸ p. 57 • WB (p. 77)

*a) Which sentences contain a participle clause? Mark the clauses.*

1 The girl driving the car didn't have a licence.

2 Teenagers threatening other people maybe need help and not punishment.

3 My dad saw a boy with a gun while he was driving past the old factory in Hill Street.

4 The kids spraying graffiti were about 13 years old.

5 Our neighbours saw two teenagers vandalizing a children's play area.

3610

6 People are moving away from our area of town because of troublemakers.

*b) Translate the clauses you have marked into German.*

1 Das Mädchen, das ______

## 11 STUDY SKILLS A written discussion ▸ p. 59 • SF (p. 154)

*a) Think of arguments for and against this statement:* **Students should not have to write tests/exams in school.** *Make notes first.*

| FOR | AGAINST |
|---|---|
| • students often don't do their best under stress | • students can't assess their work correctly without tests |
| ______________________ | ______________________ |
| ______________________ | ______________________ |
| ______________________ | ______________________ |
| ______________________ | ______________________ |
| ______________________ | ______________________ |

*b) Decide if you are for or against the statement. Then organize your arguments with an outline:*

Introduction | Presentation of arguments | Conclusion

Here are some ideas. You can add arguments or use your own ideas. Write your text in your exercise book.

| | |
|---|---|
| Introduction | *Most students hate tests and exams because they are afraid of ... But what would happen if there were no tests in school? In my experience ...* |
| Arguments for or against | *First ... because ... For example, ... Second ... Another point is that ... Finally ...* |
| Conclusion | *To sum up I think that students ... In my opinion, ... I think there are more advantages than disadvantages, so ...* |

*c)* **Extra** *Brainstorm your ideas, write notes and an outline on this topic in your exercise book:* **Can TV cause antisocial behaviour?**

## 12 REVISION What is done? (Passive: simple present/simple past) ▸ p. 60 • WB (p. 78)

*Complete what Tess says about volunteer work with the verbs in brackets in the passive, simple present or simple past.*

Young people *are needed* to do volunteer work in over a hundred countries.

Hi, my name's Tess. Young people *are needed* (need) to do volunteer work in over a hundred countries.

People always ask me what kind of work ______ (do) by volunteers. Well, everything! For example, buildings ______ (repair), the environment[1] ______ (protect), children and sick[2] people ______ (help), English ______ (teach). Last year I was in a small village called Onwe, near Kumasi in Ghana. During my four weeks there the school room *was* ______ (repair) and a children's play area ______ (build), and thanks to an environmental project a small lake in the area ______ (clean up). Volunteering is great.

3712 You know that you are giving help where it ______ (really, need).

[1] environment [ɪnˈvaɪrənmənt] *Umwelt, Natur* [2] sick [sɪk] *krank*

## 13 Volunteering in India (Passive: will-future with modals) ▸ p. 60 • WB (p. 78)

*An international group of young volunteers has arrived in a village in India, to take part in a social work camp project. The project leader gives them general information. Complete some of the things he says with sentences in the passive.*

1 You *will be divided* ________ (will – divide) into work groups of four volunteers.

2 A list of names ________ (will – put up) on the notice board in the main building.

3 Camp rules ________ (should – follow) for your own safety.

4 The camp ________ (must – keep) as clean and tidy as possible.

5 Dress code and local traditions ________ (must – respect) at all times.

6 Alcohol ________ (~~must~~ – drink) in the camp.

7 Any problems ________ (should – report) to the group leaders.

8 Changes ________ (can – make) to your programme if you aren't happy.

3813 9 The project leader ________ (should – inform) if you're ill and need a doctor.

## 14 So much has been done (Passive: present perfect) ▸ p. 61 • WB (p. 78)

*A group of young volunteers has been working on a project to repair and improve the school in a village in Uganda. This is what* **has/hasn't been done** *so far. Complete the sentences with the present perfect passive.*

1 The school building *has been painted* ________ (paint).

2 Two new classrooms ________ (add).

3 A fence ________ yet (~~build~~).

4 Trees ________ (plant).

5 A computer ________ (install).

6 A toilet ________ (build).

3814 7 The old school bus ________ yet (~~repair~~).

## 15 MEDIATION International work camps ▸ p. 61 • WB (p. 76)

*Tell a British exchange student the main facts from the following website: who takes part in the work camp programmes, how long you stay, what kind of work you do, how long you work, free-time activities, etc. Make notes in English in your exercise book first.*

**Internationale Workcamps für Teenager**

**Wer, wo und wann?**
Jedes Jahr nehmen junge Leute aus aller Welt an Hilfsprojekten in internationalen Workcamps in über hundert Ländern teil. Dabei lernen die Teilnehmer/innen nicht nur andere Länder und Kulturen kennen. Bei einem Aufenthalt von zwei bis sechs Wochen arbeiten sie zusammen an einem sinnvollen Projekt. Die Camps finden meist von Juni bis September für die Altersgruppen von 14 bis 19 Jahren statt.

**Arbeitsgruppen und Arbeitsbereiche**
In jeder Workcamp-Gruppe sind 10 bis höchstens 20 Teilnehmer/innen, die jeden Tag ca. vier Stunden mit einem/einer Gruppenleiter/in zusammenarbeiten. Die Arbeitsbereiche sind vielfältig, z.B. Umweltprojekte, Betreuung von Kindern, Englischunterricht, Mitarbeit in Krankenhäusern oder Waisenhäusern, Renovierung von Schulen, Jugendzentren und Spielplätzen oder historischen Gebäuden. Die Campsprache ist meist Englisch.

**Unterbringung und Freizeit**
Unterkünfte, z.B. in Jugendzentren oder Jugendherbergen, werden zur Verfügung gestellt. Auch die Verpflegung ist kostenfrei. Oft wird nicht nur zusammen gegessen, sondern unter Anleitung auch zusammen gekocht. Freizeitaktivitäten kommen auch nicht zu kurz. Zum Freizeitprogramm gehören nicht nur gemeinsame Ausflüge und Sightseeing, sondern auch Workshops. Viel Sport sowie Fahrradtouren und Wanderungen stehen auch auf dem Programm.

WB, pp. 65–66

## 16 READING WORKING WITH THE TEXT The caller ▸ pp. 62–64 • WB (pp. 71–72)

**a)** *How well do you know the story? Read the summary carefully. A few details are not correct. Mark the wrong sentences, sentence parts or words.*

Lindsay's Aunt Margaret has died. At the funeral Lindsay's dad loses his car keys. Later at home, when Lindsay gets a call from a voice that says it's Aunt Margaret, she thinks it's her friend Candice. Lindsay goes to Missy's party and wears the diamond earrings of her dead aunt to show off. When the voice of Aunt Margaret calls Lindsay again on her father's cellphone, Lindsay thinks it's her cousins who are playing a trick. Lindsay tells the voice that she was only nice to her because she wanted the ring. That evening all the girls stay at Missy's house. Lindsay gets a third call from the unknown caller on her father's cellphone. The voice says she's coming back to get the ring. Lindsay thinks it's her brothers again who have found the phone and are trying to scare her. Lindsay calls home, but her mom says the boys are playing cards. In the middle of the call the lights go out at Lindsay's house and there's a loud noise. Then someone knocks at the back door of Missy's house. Lindsay is scared. She wants Missy to see who is at the door. Missy leaves Lindsay alone upstairs. Then Lindsay's phone rings again. She hears footsteps on the stairs and is afraid that it's Aunt Margaret's ghost. The voice behind the bedroom door sounds like Missy's, laughing at Lindsay because she's crying like a baby. Angry with Missy, Lindsay opens the door, but it is not Missy who is holding the phone in a muddy hand ...

3917 3918

**b)** *Find at least two parts in the text that tell the reader something about Lindsay's character. Give the line numbers. What do we get to know about Lindsay? Write in your exercise book.*

*ll. 1–4 Lindsay doesn't want to be at the funeral ...*

WB, pp. 54–58

**c)** *Scary stories are often scary because things happen that can't be explained in a logical way. Find examples of this in the text. Give the line number(s) and write notes about what happens. Write in your exercise book.*

# Unit 4 Exploring cities

## 1 What do you know? ▸ pp. 74–75

*a) Read pp. 74–75 of your student's book again. Are the statements true or false? Mark a letter.*

| | True | False |
|---|---|---|
| 1 Johannesburg and Mumbai are both on the coast. | G | A |
| 2 In the past Mumbai was called Bombay. | F | U |
| 3 Johannesburg is often called 'The city of dreams'. | J | R |
| 4 Johannesburg is almost four times bigger than Mumbai. | I | A |
| 5 Mumbai's population is smaller than the population of Johannesburg. | R | K |
| 6 Films are made in Mumbai. | A | T |
| 7 You can hear Marathi and Hindi on the streets of Johannesburg. | O | A |
| 8 Sandton is a rich suburb of Mumbai. | R | N |
| 9 In Johannesburg there are lots of people without work. | S | I |

*b) If the letters you have marked are correct, they spell the name of a language:* ______

*c) Write a short profile (60–70 words) of Mumbai or Johannesburg. Use suitable facts from the fact files and the photos on pp. 74–75. You can also add interesting facts from your own research (books, internet).*

*Mumbai is a very big city on the west coast of India ... It has/There are ... Johannesburg is a big city ...*

*A short profile of*

______

______

______

______

______

## 2 WORDS Describing things and places in the city

▸ p. 78

**a)** *Which words do not fit? Mark the adjectives that you would not generally use to describe the nouns given. Then add two suitable adjectives to each list.*

1 **street markets:** exciting, colourful, glamorous, busy, ______

2 **shopping malls:** expensive, fashionable, elegant, busy, polluted, ______

3 **public transport system:** crowded, clean, financial, cheap, ______

4 **financial centres:** international, tiny, world-famous, modern, ______

5 **suburbs:** poor, rich, modern, crowded, stressful, clean, quiet, ______

6 **streets:** busy, dirty, clean, homeless, colourful, noisy, ______

**b)** *Write sentences about Mumbai and/or Johannesburg from the information on pp. 74–77 of your student's book. Use suitable adjective and noun combinations from a).*

1 *Mumbai has lots of exciting and colourful street markets.*

2 ______

3 ______

4 ______

5 ______

4102
4103
6 ______

## 3 SPEAKING Living in Mumbai

▸ p. 78

*Think about what you have read in your student's book and heard on the CD about Mumbai. Imagine living there. Write notes about the positive and negative sides for a three-minute talk in class.*

*I'm going to talk about the positive and negative sides of Mumbai. I'd like to start with ...*

| 🙂 | 🙁 |
| --- | --- |
| *friendly people,* | *noisy, busy traffic,* |
| | |
| | |
| | |
| | |
| | |
| | |
| | |

WB, pp. 63–64

4104

**INFO BOX**

A third of Mumbai's population are very poor.
By contrast, the richest people in India live in Mumbai. The city is the home of 23 billionaires!

## 4 EVERYDAY ENGLISH SPEAKING At the doctor's ▸ p. 79 14

a) *Doctor or patient? Who says what? Write **D** or **P** in the box.*

- Well, I have a pain in my knee, just here. It really hurts when I press. P
- Good morning. Thank you.
- Now, what seems to be the problem?
- Good morning. Please take a seat.
- When did the pain start? D
- Did you do any sport yesterday?
- Yesterday evening. It has got worse since then. Now I can hardly walk.
- I see. Well, I'll give you a prescription for some pills and some cream. No sport for a week and you'll be fine. OK? Goodbye.
- Yes. I played tennis for three hours in the morning. But nothing hurt then.
- Goodbye, doctor, and thank you.

b) *Put the sentences in the correct order and write the dialogue in your exercise book. Then listen to the CD (14) and check your answers.*

c) *How would you tell a doctor the following? Translate the sentences into English.*

1 Ich habe Bauchschmerzen und Fieber.

*I've got a stomach ache and a temperature.*

2 Ich habe Kopf- und Halsschmerzen.

3 Wie viele Tabletten muss ich nehmen?

4 Wie lange muss ich die Tabletten nehmen?

WB, pp. 63–64

4204
4205

## 5 MEDIATION Too much sun ▸ p. 79 • WB (p. 76)

*Here are some tips in a brochure. Read the questions below, then scan the text and tell a German friend the answers.*

1 Wann sollte man eine Sonnencreme benutzen?
2 Wann sollte man nicht in die Sonne gehen?
3 Was ist beim Schwimmen zu beachten?
4 Was ist bei Kindern zu beachten?

### PROTECTING YOUR BODY FROM SUNBURN

When you're travelling in a hot country, one of your problems may be too much sun.
When your skin starts to hurt, it's usually too late. But there are a few things you can do to protect yourself.

**Sunscreen**
Use sunscreen at least half an hour before you go in the sun. If the sun is very strong, use an SPF[1] 30. This is a must for children.

**Choose the right time to sunbathe**
Don't go in the sun at the hottest times of the day, usually between 11 am and 3 pm.
Don't sit in the direct sun. Sit under a tree or in the shade of a building or umbrella[2].

**Sun and water**
Wear a T-shirt when you go in the water.
This is very important for children.
After swimming in the sea, if possible take a shower to wash off the salt water, which dries your skin. Don't forget to use sunscreen again after your swim.

**Which clothes to wear in the sun**
When you're outdoors but not on a beach, wear long trousers, a cap or a hat and sunglasses. Cover your arms and shoulders. White and light colours are more suitable than black and dark ones.

WB, pp. 65–66

[1] Sun Protection Factor [prəˈtekʃn ˈfæktə] *Sonnenschutzfaktor* [2] umbrella [ʌmˈbrelə] *Schirm*

## 6 WRITING Which picture? ▸ p. 82 • SF (p. 135)

*Choose one of the photos and describe it in detail. Read your description in class. The class has to say which picture you have described. First say what the photo shows, for example a street scene. Then say where you can see what, how many people there are, what they are doing/wearing, etc. Write the text in your exercise book.*

*The picture that I have chosen shows ... In the foreground/background/middle you can see ...*
*On the left/right there's/there are ... A man/woman/boy/girl wearing ... is ...*
*At the top/bottom of the picture some people are ...*

## 7 WORDS Word building (Adjectives) ▸ p. 82

*Katie is in South Africa with a group of students. Complete part of her e-mail to a friend in the UK. Add the endings **-y**, **-less** or **-able** to make suitable adjectives from the words in brackets. Be careful, you need **un-** in one sentence.*

Hi Leo!
Right now we're in Johannesburg. We've seen so many _unforgettable_ (forget) sights here, and also very bad things. The tour of Soweto with a local guide was a really sad experience. We had never seen so many __________ (home) people living in slums or on the streets. I felt very sad.
Unemployment is a big problem in Johannesburg. There are thousands of __________ (job) people in the townships. In contrast, the suburb of Sandton in the north, with its glass skyscrapers, top banks, world-class hotels and restaurants, is __________ (believe). The shopping malls too – and cheaper than at home!
We've been __________ (luck) with the weather so far. Sometimes it's __________ (wind) but it's mainly __________ (sun) with a __________ (cloud) sky. It's hot but we wear __________ (suit) clothes like long trousers and hats. Mum always says too much sun isn't __________ (health)! ...

4307

## 8 Johannesburg: What do you know? ▸ p. 83

*a) Read p. 75 and pp. 80–83 of your student's book again. Then tick the correct answer, A, B or C.*

1 In Johannesburg the big problems are …

- A crime, AIDS and tsunamis. (A)
- B pollution, crime and earthquakes. (O)
- C crime, unemployment and AIDS. (L)

2 Soweto is …

- A a rich suburb. (J)
- B a poor township. (E)
- C a famous national park. (B)

3 What is Sandton?

- A A rich suburb of Johannesburg (G)
- B A township (U)
- C An animal park (R)

4 Who is Nelson Mandela?

- A The mayor of Johannesburg (G)
- B An apartheid leader (B)
- C South Africa's first black president (I)

5 During apartheid …

- A white people had disadvantages. (A)
- B there were fewer black people than white people. (G)
- C black children could not go to the same schools as whites. (O)

*b) Now write the letters after your answers in the boxes below. Johannesburg has a second name. If your answers are correct, the letters spell that name. Here are the question numbers:*

| 2 | 3 | 5 | 1 | 4 |
|---|---|---|---|---|
| | | | | |

**INFO BOX**

Johannesburg is one of the world's most important business centres for gold and diamonds. Almost half the world's gold is found in the area.
The city is also very green. People say there are more than 10 million trees in and around the city.

## 9 WRITING Visiting Germany ▸ p. 85 • WB (pp. 74–75)

*Write a short travel article for a British teen magazine giving travel tips for British teenagers in Germany. The title of your article is: 'Visiting Germany'. Think about important sights in your town/Berlin/Germany. Read also about the four things that are different on pp. 84–85 of your student's book again. Use the notes below or your own ideas.*

1 Danke = No, thanks./Yes, please.
2 In German restaurants/cafés you can choose to pay just for yourself or for everyone.
3 You can't buy stamps in German supermarkets.
4 Germans don't queue at bus stops.

*Write in your exercise book and prepare to present your article to the class. Remember:*

1 Start with a general sentence that gets your readers interested.
2 Use short topic sentences to introduce a paragraph.
3 Start a new paragraph for each new tip or topic.
4 Think of a suitable last sentence.
5 Read your completed text carefully.
6 Correct any spelling or grammar mistakes.

WB, pp. 59–62

*If you are planning to spend a holiday in Germany, there are a few things that you may like to know … One useful thing to know is that … Another thing that's different is …*

## 10 EVERYDAY ENGLISH At a hotel ▸ p. 86 🎧 15

*a) Match the receptionist's sentences to the situations below.*

Good morning. Can I help you? • Breakfast is served from 7 to 11 am. • Did you book a single or a double room? • How would you like to pay? • Would you fill in this form, please? • Here's your key card, sir/madam. • The breakfast room is on the first floor. • Did you have any extras from room service? • The lifts are over there on the right. • I hope you enjoyed your stay.

| 1 Checking in | 2 Checking out | 3 Giving information |
|---|---|---|
| Good morning. Can I help you? | | |
| | | |
| | | |
| | | |
| | | |
| | | |

*b) Complete the dialogue with suitable phrases from a). Then listen and check (🎧 15).*

*Receptionist* Good morning. Can I help you?

*Guest* Yes, my name is Robins. I booked a room for three nights.

*Receptionist* ______________________________

*Guest* A double with bathroom.

*Receptionist* Just a moment, please. Yes. We need your details, sir.

______________________________

and sign at the bottom? – Thank you. Here's ______________ . Room 239 on

the second floor. ______________________________ on the right.

*Guest* Thank you. Could you tell me when breakfast is served and where the breakfast room is?

*Receptionist* Yes, of course. ______________________________

______________________________

4510
4511

*Guest* Thank you.

## 11 LISTENING Calling reception ▸ p. 86 • WB (p. 71) 🎧 16

*Listen to the telephone calls between the hotel receptionist and three hotel guests. What do the guests want? Tick the correct box. More than one answer may be correct.*

WB, pp. 50–53

| | | | | | | |
|---|---|---|---|---|---|---|
| Guest 1: | room service | ☐ | a different room | ☐ | check out early | ☐ |
| Guest 2: | help with bags | ☐ | flight information | ☐ | a taxi to the airport | ☐ |
| Guest 3: | check out early | ☐ | breakfast in his room | ☐ | a wake-up call | ☐ |

## 12 Extra Tony would have done … (Conditional sentences 3) ▸ p. 87 • WB (p. 78)

*Tony went to Berlin with some friends. They did everything together, but Tony* ***would have done*** *some things differently. Where* ***would*** *he* ***have gone****? What* ***would*** *he* ***have done****?*

1 On the first day they went shopping. (go sightseeing)

*Tony would have gone sightseeing.*

2 On the first evening they went to a disco. (watch German TV)

_______________

3 On the second day they did a walking tour. (do a bike tour)

_______________

4 In the evenings they always ate at a pizza place. (like Turkish food)

_______________

5 On the last day of their trip they visited the Berlin zoo. (visit the Technical Museum)

4612 _______________

### Extra Now you

*If you had been on the Berlin trip with Tony and his friends, which of the things above* ***would*** *you* ***have done****? Write three to five sentences in your exercise book.*

*I think I would have visited the zoo too. I think I wouldn't have …*

## 13 WORDS Words with similar meanings ▸ p. 87

**a)** *Find words in the box with a similar meaning and write pairs.*

| | | | |
|---|---|---|---|
| connect: | *link* | similar to: | |
| maybe: | | complete: | |
| sum up: | | difference: | |
| immediately: | | discuss: | |
| mostly: | | find: | |

at once • contrast • discover • talk about • finish • like • *link* • mainly • perhaps • summarize

**b)** *Underline the word in each sentence that you can change. Then use a word from a) with a similar meaning.*

1 We talked about the history of apartheid in school today. *discussed*

2 Gold was found in South Africa in 1885. _______________

3 The population of Johannesburg is mostly black African. _______________

4 The big difference between rich and poor people is shocking. _______________

5 Maybe I'll do a presentation about Johannesburg. _______________

4613 6 At the end of your talk, don't forget to summarize your main points. _______________

## 14 SPEAKING COURSE Part 4: A talk about Johannesburg (Giving a presentation) ▸ p. 88 • WB (p. 73)

**a)** *These sentences are from a student's presentation about Johannesburg. Put them in the correct order 2–9.*

| | |
|---|---|
| To sum up my presentation, we have seen that Johannesburg is a city of great contrasts with an interesting history. | ____ |
| My topic today is 'Johannesburg: past and present'. | 1 |
| Would anybody like to ask any questions or make comments? | ____ |
| After that I'd like to look at the history of Johannesburg. | ____ |
| I've divided my presentation into four sections. | ____ |
| Finally, I'd like to present some slides of typical city sights. | ____ |
| In the third section I'll describe the city's present problems. | ____ |
| I'll begin with some general facts about the city's population. | ____ |
| If there are no more questions, I'd like to thank you for listening. | ____ |

*Nelson Mandela, a South African hero*

**b)** *In your exercise book, write a paragraph that you would put in one of the main sections in a). Choose from: 1) general facts 2) Johannesburg's history 3) the city's present problems. You can use information from p. 75 and pp. 80–83 in your student's book.*

## 15 STUDY SKILLS Visual materials ▸ p. 88

**a)** *How many visual materials do you know? Write a list.*

pictures, ____________________

Why is it good to use visual materials in your presentations?

They make your presentation ____________________

____________________

____________________

**b)** *Make a pie chart which you could use in the presentation on Johannesburg. For example, the chart could show the different ethnic groups in the city.*

73% Blacks ☐
16% Whites ☐
6% Other ☐
4% Asians ☐

**c)** *What phrases could you use to talk about the pie chart you have made?*

Here is a pie chart of ... It shows that ... ____________________

____________________

## Now You

WB, pp. 63–64

*With the information from exercises 14 and 15 prepare a talk about Johannesburg. Practise your talk and present it in class.*

## 16 WORDS Unit 4 puzzle ▸ p. 88

*Write the answers in the puzzle and find the word in the blue boxes.*

1 English is one of the many ... languages in South Africa. 1 _ _ _ _ _ _ _ _
2 You have to show this when you enter a foreign country. 2 _ _ _ _ _ _ _ _
3 The old name for Mumbai is ... 3 _ _ _ _ _ _
4 The richest ... of Johannesburg is called Sandton. 4 _ _ _ _ _ _
5 A main problem in many big cities is ... 5 _ _ _ _ _ _ _ _ _
6 One of the main languages in Mumbai is ... 6 _ _ _ _ _
7 Many South Africans think Nelson Mandela is a ... 7 _ _ _ _
8 The 'Soweto ...' took place on 16th June, 1976. 8 _ _ _ _ _ _ _ _
4816 9 The informal word for a large room in a hostel or school where many people can sleep. 9 _ _ _ _

## 17 My book quiz ▸ p. 88

*How well do you know your student's book? Here you can test yourself. Give short answers.*

1 The capital of Australia is ______
2 The name of the famous rock that is important to Aboriginal culture is ______
3 Name three Australian animals. ______
4 What do Australians call their kind of football? ______
5 The paper that tells others about your education and work experience is called your ______
6 When you apply for a job, you should also send a letter of ______
7 The time when you train for a job is called an ______
8 UK courts don't always send young troublemakers to prison. They give them ______
9 In the US troublemakers can choose to go to ... instead of[1] prison. ______
10 Which city has the biggest population: Mumbai or Johannesburg? ______
4818 11 Soweto is a famous township in which city? ______
4819 12 What is the name of India's film industry? ______

[1] instead of [ɪn'sted] *anstelle von*

## How well can you do these things?

| | Very well | OK | Practise! |
|---|---|---|---|
| **LISTENING AND READING SKILLS: I can …** | | | |
| … read longer fictional and non-fictional texts without difficulty, e.g. *The caller*, (SB pp. 62–63). | ☐ | ☐ | ☐ |
| … follow a class presentation. | ☐ | ☐ | ☐ |
| **SPEAKING AND WRITING SKILLS: I can …** | | | |
| … structure, prepare and give a presentation, e.g. about Berlin. | ☐ | ☐ | ☐ |
| … take part in a discussion, express my opinion, give reasons and examples, agree and disagree, e.g. about boot camps. | ☐ | ☐ | ☐ |
| … describe and compare two photos. | ☐ | ☐ | ☐ |
| … have a conversation with a doctor about an illness or accident. | ☐ | ☐ | ☐ |
| … write an outline for a written discussion, with arguments and examples for and against a statement and then sum up the main points with my personal opinion, e.g. on community service. | ☐ | ☐ | ☐ |
| … write a formal letter to the editor of a magazine giving my opinion about an article I have read, e.g. about the use of mobile phones. | ☐ | ☐ | ☐ |
| **MEDIATION SKILLS: I can …** | | | |
| … summarize and report a conversation or written text from German into English or from English into German, e.g. about volunteer work. | ☐ | ☐ | ☐ |
| … use my own words when I summarize. I do not translate the original conversation or written text. | ☐ | ☐ | ☐ |
| **TOPICS: I have learned …** | | | |
| … about the problems of big cities like Mumbai, Johannesburg and Berlin, e.g. pollution, crime, unemployment and overcrowding. | ☐ | ☐ | ☐ |
| … about apartheid in South Africa and what it meant for black citizens. | ☐ | ☐ | ☐ |
| … about teenage activities, interests and hobbies, e.g. mobile phone behaviour, volunteer work and community service. | ☐ | ☐ | ☐ |
| … about problems of teenagers who behave antisocially and about punishments for antisocial behaviour, e.g. ASBOs and boot camps. | ☐ | ☐ | ☐ |
| **STUDY AND LANGUAGE SKILLS: I know …** | | | |
| … how to create visual materials, e.g. posters, overhead transparencies, maps, charts and timelines and I can use them in presentations. | ☐ | ☐ | ☐ |

**WAYS TO IMPROVE MY ENGLISH SKILLS: I could …**

(work through Skills Check 2 again, revise the unit vocabulary in my student's book …)

______________________________

______________________________

______________________________

______________________________

# LISTENING

*In this part of your workbook you will find exercises that will help you with your skills: listening, reading, writing, speaking, mediation.*

## 1 Chat in the break (Listening for gist) ▸ *WB (p. 71)* 17

*Listen to four short dialogues. What are the friends talking about? Match the letters to the topic.*

| | |
|---|---|
| A | A project |
| B | A school trip |
| C | Weekend plans |
| D | The school team |

**Tip 1**

Look at the four topics. **Which words/ word fields** might you expect to hear? Listen for those words.
For example:
**project** > *research, subject, finish*
**school trip** > *bus/train, place, time*
**weekend plans** > *friends, party*
**school team** > *match, game, play*

## 2 The Olympic Games (Listening for gist) 18

*Read statements A–E. Then listen to four students talking about the Olympic Games. Match the statements to the students. Write the correct letter in the box. There is one statement/letter that you do not need.*

A I'm a sporty person, so I love the summer Olympics.
B I think the Olympic Games have become too political.
C The Games have become too spectacular and too expensive.
D I'm not into sport, so I don't really follow the Games on TV.
E We can all learn a lot from Olympic athletes.

5002 Student 1: ☐ Student 2: ☐ Student 3: ☐ Student 4: ☐

**Tip 2**

Before you listen, concentrate[1] on the statements A–E.
Decide which are **positive** and which are **negative**. Mark **key words** and listen for them.
Notice how the speakers give their opinion. Is their **tone** of voice positive or negative?

## 3 Tricky numbers, times, letters (Listening for detail) ▸ *WB (p. 71)* 19

*Listen to the CD and mark what you hear: one of each pair.*

*a) Numbers:* 245 / 254 | 14 / 40 | 98 / 89 | 60 / 16 | 02256691 / 02256651 | 1978 / 1987

*b) Times:* 2.30 / 2.13 | 12.30 / 1.30 | 4.30 / 3.30 | 9.15 / 9.50

5003 *c) Letters:* A / E | E / I | A / R | G / J | J / G

**Tip 3**

When you listen the first time, write down **names**, **places**, **dates**, **numbers**, **times** or **letters**. When you listen a second time, check your notes and concentrate on the answers you still need.

## 4 At the station (Listening for detail) ▸ *WB (p. 71)* 20

*You are going to hear three short train announcements. First read the statements below carefully. Then listen to the announcements and tick the correct box.*

| | | True | False |
|---|---|---|---|
| 1 | The train to Edinburgh will leave from platform 6. | ☐ | ☐ |
| 2 | The train will leave 13 minutes later. | ☐ | ☐ |
| 3 | The 12.15 train to Bristol will not leave from platform 9 today. | ☐ | ☐ |
| 4 | The Bristol train will now leave from platform 7E. | ☐ | ☐ |
| 5 | The train from York will now arrive at platform 3 at 12.43. | ☐ | ☐ |

5004

**Tip 4**

Look carefully at the **details** in the questions, for example, prepositions: *from, to, at*. Then listen for them. For example, did you hear 'from' or 'to'?

[1] concentrate on sth. ['kɒnsntreɪt] *sich auf etw. konzentrieren*

## 5 The London Eye (Listening for detail) ▸ *WB (p. 71)* 🎧 21

*Listen to a guide telling tourists about the London Eye. Then tick the correct answer, A, B or C.*

1 The tourists' ride on the Eye is booked[1] for …

A 2.30 pm. B 3.30 pm. C 4.30 pm.

2 How far can you see on a clear day?

A 40 miles. B 40 kilometres. C 14 kilometres.

3 When did work on the London Eye start?

A 1990. B 1991. C 1992.

4 How many passenger[2] capsules[3] are there?

A 23. B 25. C 32.

5105 5 The London Eye is now the … biggest wheel in the world.

A second B third C fourth

**Tip 5**

Often information is given **indirectly**. For example:
*When did work on the Eye start?*
You hear only:
*It took 7 years to build and it was opened in 1999.* You can work out the answer from this information.

## 6 BE and AE (BE and AE pronunciation) ▸ *WB (p. 71)* 🎧 22–24

**a)** *Listen to the words (🎧 22). Is the pronunciation BE or AE? Write A (American) or B (British) in the box. If you are not sure, listen again.*

1 ☐ 5 ☐ 9 ☐
2 ☐ 6 ☐ 10 ☐
3 ☐ 7 ☐ 11 ☐
5106 4 ☐ 8 ☐ 12 ☐

**Tip 6**

| | BE | AE |
|---|---|---|
| *grass, can't* | [ɑː] | [æ] |
| *knew, Tuesday* | [juː] | [uː] |
| *not, got* | [ɒ] | [ɑ] |
| *first, world, more* > | in AE you hear the 'r' | |
| *little, city, writer* > | in AE 't' in the middle of a word sounds like 'd' | |

**b)** *Now look carefully at the following sentences. Mark the sounds which are pronounced differently in AE. Then listen and check that you have marked all the differences (🎧 23). You'll hear each sentence twice: first in BE, then in AE.*

1 It's so hot in here! Let's go to the park! I'll ask my sister if she wants to join us.

2 Let's have a nice cool drink first. How about a glass of mineral water? Or some coffee?

3 I forgot to tell you. We have a new student in our class. It's her birthday soon.

She's invited us all to a party.

**c)** *You're in a tourist information office in London. Listen to what the people are asking (🎧 24). Are they British or American? Write the number of each speaker under the UK or the US flag.*

Speakers ______________________

Speakers 1, ______________________

[1] book [bʊk] *buchen* [2] passenger [ˈpæsɪndʒə] *Passagier, Fahrgast* [3] capsule [ˈkæpsjuːl] *Kapsel*

## 7 At the youth hostel (Accents) ▸ *WB (p. 71)* 25

*You hear some young people talking about why tourists like to visit their countries. Do they come from the* **UK**, *the* **USA** *or* **Australia**? *Write the country under the photo.*

5207 *1* ________ *2* ________ *3* ________ *4* ________ *5* ________ *6* ________

## 8 In a café (Fast speech) ▸ *WB (p. 71)* 26, 27

*a) Listen to three teenagers talking about their problems (26). They talk at a normal speed[1], but in everyday speech some words are shortened or missed out. You will hear some of the short forms in* **Tip 7**. *Who says what? Write the names in 1–4 below.* **Todd, Will or Liz**?

*1* ________ and ________ are having problems with parents.

*2* ________ 's parents are not as strict with his younger brother.

*3* ________ doesn't know how to solve[3] his problem with his girlfriend.

*4* ________ is having problems with her grades at school.

**Tip 7**

When people talk **quickly**, they may use words or phrases that are not grammatically correct. You hear the following forms especially[2] in AE. Maybe you've heard these forms in song lyrics too:

*gonna > going to*
*wanna > want to*
*gotta > have got to*
*kinda > kind of*
*dunno > don't know*

*b) Listen to the rest of the conversation (27). This time the friends talk faster. Listen carefully and tick true or false.*

| | True | False |
|---|---|---|
| *1* Liz doesn't want to give up her weekend job. | ☐ | ☐ |
| *2* Liz thinks she'll talk to her Math teacher and her Science teacher. | ☐ | ☐ |
| *3* Will's girlfriend is called Katie. | ☐ | ☐ |
| *4* Will doesn't always work on Friday evenings. | ☐ | ☐ |
| *5* Will has a job at a pizza place. | ☐ | ☐ |
| *6* Will has a friend called Matt. | ☐ | ☐ |
| *7* Will's girlfriend went to a movie with a boy called Stevie. | ☐ | ☐ |
| *8* Todd says Will has to trust[4] his girlfriend more. | ☐ | ☐ |

[1] speed [spiːd] *Geschwindigkeit* [2] especially [ɪˈspeʃəli] *besonders* [3] solve [sɒlv] *lösen* [4] trust [trʌst] *vertrauen*

## 9 Talking about jobs (Listening skills) ▸ *WB (p. 71)* 28

***a)*** *Listen to five young people talking about jobs. First, read the statements below and the list of names. Then listen to what they say. Choose the correct statement below for each person. Write A–E next to the names.*

A 'I've found a job as a waitress in a café, but I won't find out details until I call again later today.'

B 'I had a big problem on my first day. The manager wasn't very happy.'

C 'I've applied for lots of jobs I got from the job centre. I've had one job offer so far.'

D 'I enjoy my work now, but at first I wasn't allowed to serve customers because I had to learn the job.'

E 'I wanted to work with computers, but I'm learning to repair cars now. I like it.'

*1* Dylan: ☐ *2* Sophie: ☐ *3* Gina: ☐ *4* Jamie: ☐ *5* Leo: ☐

***b)*** *Now listen again, this time for detail. Choose the correct answer and tick the box.*

*1* Dylan is looking for ...

☐ a summer job. ☐ a job after school. ☐ a Saturday job.

*2* Dylan found some jobs at the job centre, and he has applied for ...

☐ four. ☐ five. ☐ six.

*3* Sophie already has some job experience ...

☐ in a hotel. ☐ in a café. ☐ in a restaurant.

*4* Sophie has to call again about the job at ...

☐ 1.30. ☐ 2.30. ☐ 3.30.

*5* Gina is from ...

☐ Australia. ☐ the UK. ☐ the USA.

*6* Gina works in a flower[1] shop ...

☐ from nine to five. ☐ from nine to six. ☐ after school.

*7* Jamie has a ...

☐ part-time job. ☐ holiday job. ☐ full- time job.

*8* Jamie works in ...

☐ Glasgow. ☐ Aberdeen. ☐ a village near Aberdeen.

*9* Leo has been working in a travel agency[2] ...

☐ for a week. ☐ for a month. ☐ since he left school.

*10* Leo sent the wrong flight tickets to Mrs White. She wanted to go to ...

☐ Johannesburg. ☐ Hawaii. ☐ Alaska.

[1] flower [flaʊə] *Blume* [2] travel agency ['eɪdʒənsi] *Reisebüro*

# READING

## 10 ESL in L.A. (1) (Skimming) ▸ *WB (p. 71)*

*You would like to visit L. A. and maybe do an English course. You find this information on the internet. Would it be useful to you? Who is the information for? Skim the text for a few seconds. Then tick A, B or C.*

The information is for … [A] American college students. [B] teachers of ESL. [C] foreign students of English.

| English as a second language (ESL) in L.A. | |
|---|---|
| **ESL programs** | Our programs cover all areas of English as a second language. We offer **intensive programs** and exam preparation programs for college and university entrance. |
| **Course levels** | We offer courses for beginners, intermediate and advanced levels[1]. All levels provide[2] training in reading, listening, speaking and writing skills, vocabulary building, pronunciation and grammar. Courses in **American culture**, English for **business** and **commerce**, English for **science** and **technology** are offered at intermediate and advanced levels only. |
| **Course hours** | 9 am–12 am, 2 pm–5 pm or 6 pm–9 pm, Mon–Fri. There are no weekend courses. |
| **Course groups** | **Intensive programs**: groups of 6–8 students. All other course groups: 12–15 students. |
| **Teaching staff** | All our teachers are college and university trained professionals and are native speakers. |
| **Location** | Centrally located close to city attractions, shopping and eating within walking distance. |
| **Accommodation**[3] | Students may choose to stay with a selected **host**[4] **family** or at a **residence club**, (single room with breakfast and dinner). |

**Tip 8**

Step *1*: Look at the **form** of the text. Is it a newspaper article, a short story or an information brochure?

Step *2*: Look at the **title**, **headings** and **pictures**.

Step *3*: Look at the words in **bold** type.

5410

## 11 ESL in L.A. (2) (Scanning) ▸ *WB (p. 72)*

*Now scan the text in exercise 10 above to find the answers to the questions below. The key words are in **bold**. Write short answers.*

1 What does '**ESL**' mean? ______

2 How many **course levels** are offered? ______

3 Do all courses teach **American culture**? ______

4 **Where** is the school? ______

5 Are there any courses at the **weekend**? ______

6 How many students are there in the **intensive** programs? ______

7 How many kinds of **accommodation** does the school help with? ______

8 Can students stay with a host family and have their **own room**? ______

5411

**Tip 9**

Concentrate only on the **key words** in the questions when you scan. Read **around** a key word to find the answer. Remember, you may find a key word in one or more places in the text.

[1] advanced level [əd'vɑːnsd 'levl] *fortgeschrittenes Niveau* [2] provide [prə'vaɪd] *bieten* [3] accomodation [əˌkɒmə'deɪʃn] *Unterkunft* [4] host [həʊst] *Gastgeber/in*

## 12 Getting into London (Marking key words, taking notes) ▸ WB (p. 72)

*a) You are flying to London, so you need information about different kinds of transport into London from Heathrow Airport. Choose and mark key words for the most important details.*

### Getting into London from Heathrow

From Heathrow Airport you can take a train, the tube, a coach[1] or a taxi into London.

1 If you want to go by train, the Heathrow Express takes you to Paddington Station in just 15–20 minutes. Trains run every 15 minutes. Cost: £ 16.50.
2 By tube the journey takes 45 minutes. Heathrow is on the Piccadilly line. There are three tube stations at the airport serving different terminals. The tube stops at famous places in the capital such as Hyde Park Corner, Piccadilly Circus and Covent Garden. Tube trains leave every five minutes. Cost: £4.50.
3 You can take the National Express coach from the Central Bus Station (near Terminals 1, 2 and 3) to Victoria Coach Station in central London. The journey by coach takes 45–75 minutes. There are three to six buses an hour. Cost: £5.
4 By taxi the journey takes 30–75 minutes. Cost for up to five passengers[2]: £40–70.

(Prices: February 2010)

*b) From your key words, write notes about the different kinds of transport.*

1 train: Heathrow Express > Paddington, 15–20 min., every 15 min., £16.50

2 ______

3 ______

4 ______

## 13 Florida's Marine Park (Reading for detail) ▸ WB (p. 72)

*Before you scan the text about Marine Park, read the statements on the next page. Mark the key words in the statements then look for the answers and tick true, false or not given on the next page.*

**Tip 10**

If there are no or not many words in **bold** in the text, choose your own **key words** from the questions. Look for them when you scan the text and read **around** them to find the answers.

**Opening times**
Marine Park is open to visitors every day from 9 am to 7 pm, and from 9 am to 9 pm in the summer months and at holiday times.

**How to get here**
If you are driving, you will find us just 10 miles northwest of downtown Tampa. From Tampa International Airport it is just a 20-minute taxi ride. Our main gates and car park for 3,500 vehicles are on South Marine Drive. You can't miss us! Please visit our website for detailed directions.

**Admission**
1-day tickets: Adults $83.95 (plus tax[3]), children 3–10 years $69.95 (plus tax). Children two years and under go free. There are discounts for senior citizens.
Online tickets: For tickets bought online 7 days before your visit, there is a standard price of $69.95 (plus tax). You can print your ticket at home and there's no waiting at the park entrance.

Florida visitors: Please see our special online offers for 1-day and 3-day tickets.
Florida residents[4]: Please see our special annual and vacation offers.

5513

[1] coach *Reisebus* [2] passenger ['pæsɪndʒə(r)] *Passagier/Fahrgast* [3] tax [tæks] *Steuer* [4] resident ['rezɪdənt] *Einwohner/in*

| | True | False | Not given |
|---|---|---|---|
| *1* The park is open all year round from 9 am to 9 pm. | ☐ | ☐ | ☐ |
| *2* Marine Park is ten miles northwest of Tampa. | ☐ | ☐ | ☐ |
| *3* It's a 30-minute drive from Tampa International Airport. | ☐ | ☐ | ☐ |
| *4* You enter Marine Park from South Marine Drive. | ☐ | ☐ | ☐ |
| *5* Adult tickets are cheaper online. | ☐ | ☐ | ☐ |
| *6* There is no US tax on tickets. | ☐ | ☐ | ☐ |
| *7* You can use online tickets for one year. | ☐ | ☐ | ☐ |
| *8* There are special ticket offers for Florida residents. | ☐ | ☐ | ☐ |
| *9* You can buy Quick Queue tickets. | ☐ | ☐ | ☐ |
| *10* Tickets for children under three years of age are free. | ☐ | ☐ | ☐ |

## 14 Marine Park visitor information (Reading for detail) ▸ *WB (p. 72)*

*Read the visitor information sign carefully. You don't have to understand all the words when you read the first time. Complete the sentences below with words from the text.*

**Marine Park Visitor Information**

Welcome to Marine Park. Before visitors enter the park, all bags will be examined by our security staff. It is not permitted[1] to bring sharp[2] or dangerous objects into the park, including pocket knives, cans and glass bottles. Please leave these objects in your vehicle.

Visitors are asked not to bring food and drinks into the park. Restaurants and stands selling snacks and soft drinks can be found in several areas of the park.

All indoor areas of the park are smoke-free. Outdoor smoking areas are clearly marked on your park map. If you wish to smoke, please do so in these areas only.

Information about animal feeding times can be found in the park map. Please do not try to feed the animals. It's bad for them and may be dangerous for you.

If you wish to bring along your pets, they can wait for you in our pets' area near the main gates. We ask you to walk your dog regularly during your park visit and to bring along enough pet food. Your pets will be safe and well looked after.
Our service costs just $12 a day.

For safety reasons, visitors are not allowed to take objects into the park which are ____________ or ______________ . You can buy soft drinks and snacks in the park, so you are asked not to bring your own ________ ______________ . ____________ is only permitted in some areas.

**Tip 11**

The words in the task are often different from the words in the text. But the meaning is the same.
Work out the meaning of **unknown words** from the context, for example: *examine, cans, vehicle.*

Please follow the signs. Information about ____________________ can be found in the ______________ . There's also a service that looks after visitors' __________ , so you can bring along your dog or cat too – for just $12 a day.

[1] permit [pəˈmɪt] *erlauben, gestatten* [2] sharp [ʃɑːp] *scharf*

## 15 What does it mean? (Working out the meaning of words) ▸ *WB (p. 71)*

*Look at the text in exercise 14 again. How did you work out the meaning of unknown words? Write the words in the lists with their German meaning. If a word fits into two lists, decide what helped you most.*

examined • security • staff • including • vehicle • object • stand • several • indoor • service

| … from the context | | … like a German word | | … from a part of the word or the word family | |
|---|---|---|---|---|---|
| staff | Personal | | | | |
| | | | | | |
| | | | | | |
| | | | | | |
| | | | | | |
| | | | | | |

5715

## 16 Saving our planet (Reading skills) ▸ *WB (pp. 71–72)*

*Read this section of a text about the earth's problems. You don't have to understand all the words the first time you read.*

### Saving our planet

1 Climate change is thought by scientists to be a major problem. In less than a hundred years from now, the earth's average temperature could have risen by as much as five degrees. People living in cold countries may like the idea, but the temperature rise would put the earth and its peoples in danger, as a warmer climate would have disastrous effects on the future of man and nature.

2 A main cause is that humans produce 'greenhouse gases', for example, when burning oil, gas or wood for energy. Industries are a major cause of this. CO2 is released into the atmosphere. This leads to the 'greenhouse effect', as the sun's heat is trapped by too many greenhouse gases in the atmosphere, so the earth gets warmer. Deforestation is another cause, as forests and rainforests absorb CO2.

3 The effects of global warming could be catastrophic. The ice at the poles could melt, so sea levels would rise – maybe by up to two metres in the next 150 years, some experts believe. This would mean that cities like New York, London or Tokyo might slowly disappear under the sea. Millions of people could be permanently homeless. Some countries could become seriously overpopulated. There may be more natural disasters, like tsunamis and tornadoes. Tropical diseases would spread more quickly into non-tropical countries. The heat could dry up the food we grow. Food prices would rise and millions could become hungry. There might not be enough drinking water, so wars might start. Some animals and plants might die out because they could not survive in saltwater.

4 In order to slow down climate change, we must reduce global warming, for example, by using less energy in our daily lives. We should stop burning oil and gas, which produce carbon dioxide and are non-renewable. We should use more renewable energy like solar or wind power. We should save electricity and water, and produce less waste by recycling. We could buy recyclable and energy-efficient products (light bulbs, fridges, computers, etc.). We could plant more trees. We must stop cutting down rainforests. All this and much more …

*a) Choose a suitable heading for each paragraph. Write A–D.*

| | | | | | |
|---|---|---|---|---|---|
| Paragraph 1: | | Paragraph 3: | | A Solutions[1] | C Consequences |
| Paragraph 2: | | Paragraph 4: | | B Problems | D Reasons |

*b) Look at the text again. How can you work out the meaning of the unknown words? Write the following words in lists 1–3 with their German meaning. Some words fit into two lists. Decide what helped you most.*

climate • scientist • release • greenhouse effect • heat • trapped • deforestation • poles • melt • level • disaster • tropical • dry up • saltwater • reduce • renewable • recyclable • waste • energy-efficient

1 I can understand these words from the **context**: ______

2 These words are like **German** words: ______

3 I know part of these words or a word from the **word family**: ______

*c) Read the statements below carefully. Is the information true, false or not in the text? Tick a box.*

| | True | False | Not in the text |
|---|---|---|---|
| 1 At the end of this century the earth's temperature could be a few degrees warmer. | | | |
| 2 Households produce about a third of carbon dioxide emissions. | | | |
| 3 CO2 is a 'greenhouse gas'. | | | |
| 4 Natural gas is a renewable source of energy. | | | |
| 5 A lot of the waste that we produce every day finds its way into the seas and oceans. | | | |
| 6 Recyclable products help to reduce waste. | | | |
| 7 Rainforests are burned down so that cattle farmers can produce more meat for export. | | | |
| 8 CO2 cannot be absorbed. | | | |

*d) Now complete these sentences with information from the text.*

1 Climate change is thought to be a major problem because a warmer climate could ______

2 We all produce 'greenhouse gases' by ______

3 The earth gets warmer because the sun's heat is trapped by ______

4 If the ice at the poles melted, ______. As a result, cities like ______

5 People would not have enough to eat because the heat could ______

[1] solution [sə'lu:ʃn] *Lösung*

## 17 Collecting ideas (Brainstorming) ▸ WB (pp. 74–75)

**a)** *Choose three topics from A–F below. Brainstorm ideas that you could use, for example, in an e-mail to a friend. Make a list or a mind map for each of your three topics in your exercise book.*

| | | | |
|---|---|---|---|
| A | My free time | D | Work experience |
| B | A great holiday | E | My best birthday |
| C | My ideal job | F | Raising money for homeless people |

A great holiday
2 sightseeing:
historic buildings
~~museums~~ ...
1 making new friends:
disco
pool
beach ...

**Tip 12**

Remember to cross out ideas you won't use and number the useful ideas.

**b)** *Use your notes from a) to write an e-mail to an American friend about one of your topics. Write 80–100 words in your exercise book.*

Hi ...!
Thanks for the mail and the cool photos of your trip to Miami. You wanted to know about my holiday in ... It was great too, so I'll tell you about it.
Well, ...

## 18 Giving information (The 5 Ws) ▸ WB (pp. 74–75)

**a)** *Whatever kind of text you write, your reader needs basic facts. Who or what is the text about? What happens? When, where and why does it happen? The text below is about a traffic accident. In what order does it answer the 5 Ws? Make notes below.*

**Tip 13**

The **5 Ws** are important both in reading and writing. In a good story/report, etc, you find answers to most of the *5 Ws* in the first two or three sentences. *Why ...?* and *How ...?* sometimes come later. The order of the information is not important and is usually different from text to text.

**Teenager hit by cyclist[1]**

At 10.30 last night a 15-year-old girl was hurt by a cyclist as she was crossing Radfield Road on her way home after visiting a friend. The cyclist, who admitted[2] that he was riding very fast on the empty road, ran into the girl, who was wearing dark clothes. The cyclist said, 'She came from nowhere. I just didn't see her.' The cyclist called an ambulance and the girl was treated[3] for a broken finger and shock.

1 When? at 10.30 last night

2 _____

3 _____

4 _____

5918 5 _____

**b)** *Now write a short text about your last school trip. Give information about the 5 Ws in the first few sentences, as in the text in a).* **Who** *went (students, teachers),* **where** *you went,* **when** *you went,* **how** *you got there,* **what** *you did there. Write 60–80 words in your exercise book.*

Last year ... our class went on a trip to ... with ... / Our last class trip took place in ... this year ...

[1] cyclist ['saɪklɪst] *Radfahrer/in* [2] admit [əd'mɪt] *zugeben* [3] treat [triːt] *behandeln*

## 19 Making changes

**Tip 14**

You can:
- change active to passive or passive to active.
- add a subordinate clause.
- change direct to indirect speech.
- make one sentence out of two using a linking word.
- change the linking word (e.g. *so* > *because*, *but* > *although*).

**a)** *Here are some tips that will help you when you want to write a text. Read* **Tip 14** *and study the following examples carefully.*

1 After three days the police caught the escaped prisoner. They had been told where they could find him.
Change active to passive and passive to active.
The escaped prisoner was caught after a few days. Someone had told the police where to find him.

2 It was a cold day in winter when Leila packed her bags and left home to start a new life in Pakistan. She had never met the man she was going to marry.
Add a relative clause – *where* ... , and make one sentence out of two.
On a cold winter day Leila left home for Pakistan, where she would start a new life with a husband she had never met.

3 'I'll never be able to wear jeans and tops again, no trainers either,' Leila thought sadly.
Change direct to indirect speech. Use group words not details – *western clothes for jeans, tops, trainers.*
Leila was sad that she would never be able to wear western clothes again.

4 After breakfast, Rob and Pete started their bike tour. The sun was shining. There was a warm breeze and only a few white clouds in the sky.
Make one sentence out of two with a linking word, here: *When* ... Leave out details of weather description.
The weather was very good when Rob and Pete started their cycle tour in the morning.

5 Tom always needs money, so he does a newspaper round before school and he sometimes works in his cousin's café on Wilmore Street. He washes cars and does garden work for the neighbours too.
Change the linking word – *so* > *because*. Leave out unimportant details of jobs.
Tom does lots of jobs before and after school because he always needs money.

**b)** *Now write the following sentences differently and shorten them where possible. Make one sentence. Remember to use what you have learned in a) above.*

1 It was really cold in the house, so Polly made a big pot of hot tea for everybody.

*Polly made* ______________________________

2 US border police send back hundreds of illegal Mexican immigrants every week. Pedro was one of them.

*Pedro was* ______________________________

______________________________

3 Jerry arrived late at the airport because of a traffic jam on the motorway. He found that his plane to Vancouver had already left.

*When* ______________________________

______________________________

4 'There's so much to prepare before the visitors arrive – the flat to clean, shopping to do, food to cook,' thought Emily nervously.

*Emily was nervous* ______________________________

______________________________

## 20 Writing a formal letter

▸ SF (p. 153)

***a)*** *Complete the text with words and phrases that are suitable for formal letters. If you need help, look in your student's book (p. 153).*

You put your own address ___at the top on the right___, but you don't write your name. Under your address you write ______________. The address of the person you are writing to is written ________________.

You begin a formal letter with ______________________ when you don't know the name of the person you are writing to. Remember that the first word of the first paragraph starts with a _____________ letter – which is different from German. You shouldn't use ___________ forms in formal letters. Write 'I am' and 'I would' instead of[1] 'I'm' and 'I'd'.

You finish a formal letter with _____________________ if you don't know the name of the person you are writing to. If you know the name, you start with ______________________ and you finish with ____________________.

***b)*** *Lisa Schneider from Munich is writing a letter of application for a job as assistant receptionist[2] at a hotel in London for six weeks over the summer. What belongs where in a formal letter? Choose the correct parts from the list on the right and write the number in the correct place in the letter below.*

6120

1. Best wishes
2. Yours faithfully
3. Dear Mrs Wilson
4. 2nd May 2010
5. Dear Sir or Madam
6. I look forward to hearing from you.
7. I am writing to apply for the job of assistant receptionist as advertised on your website ...
8. Webergasse 8
   81735 Munich
9. The Manager
   Lancaster Hall Hotel
   28 Lancaster Road
   London W8 IJL

**Tip 15**

**British addresses:**
Note that the house number comes **before** the name of the road or street, not after it.
Note also that in the UK the postcode comes **after** the town or city, not before it.

***c)*** *If you wanted this job, how would you write your letter of application? Write the main text of your letter in your exercise book. Write about the following:*

- your age, personal details
- how long you have been learning English and how good your English is
- what kind of person you are, work experience, your hobbies and interests
- why you would like the job and why you think you could do it well.

[1] instead of [ɪn'sted] *anstelle von* [2] receptionist [rɪ'sepʃənɪst] *Rezeptionist/in*

## 21 Writing a CV ▸ SF (p. 152)

*Lisa has to enclose her CV with the application. Here is the necessary information about her:*

Her telephone number is 0049 89 612 37 97. Her mobile number is 0049 173 835 2380.
Her e-mail is: lschneider@afl.com
She was born in Munich on 23rd November 1995.
Lisa is a friendly, hard-working student who likes speaking English and enjoys meeting people. She is good at organizing and likes working in a team. She is punctual and reliable.
She has already worked in a hotel in Rosenheim for two weeks, where she spoke English and German to hotel guests. Last year in the Easter holidays she also worked at the information desk in a shopping mall in Munich.
In her free time she likes reading and writing to online friends in the UK and the USA. She enjoys cooking, swimming and playing football.
Lisa was at primary school in Augsburg from 2001 to 2005. She has been at secondary school in Munich since 2005. She is taking her school-leaving exams (similar to GCSEs) this year. She has a good level of English (6 years) and French (4 years). She also has good computer skills and a moped licence.

***a)*** *In what order should Lisa present this information at the top of her CV? Write the numbers 1–4 behind the headings.*

| | | | |
|---|---|---|---|
| Postal address | | E-mail address | |
| Name | | Mobile number | |

**Tip 16**

Date and place of birth are not always given in English CVs, but it is useful for employers[1] to know your **age** and your **native language**.
The personal statement should not be longer than three short sentences. Use only long verb forms.

***b)*** *What could Lisa write in her short personal statement?*

___

___

___

***c)*** *In which order should she give details about the following? Write 1–6.*

| | | | | | |
|---|---|---|---|---|---|
| Work experience | | Hobbies and interests | | Education | |
| Qualifications | | Reference(s) | | Other skills | |

***d)*** *Now use the information about Lisa from the blue box above to write the CV sections in c). Leave out 'Reference(s)'. Remember to write in note form, not in full sentences.*

Education: 2001 – 2005

___

___

___

___

___

___

___

6221

***e)*** *Write Lisa's CV on the computer using the correct format.*

[1] employer [ɪmˈplɔɪə(r)] *Arbeitgeber/in*

# SPEAKING

## 22 Asking for information (Question forms) ▸ WB (pp. 72–73) 29

*When you ask for information, it is important to form questions correctly and quickly. How do the teenagers ask the questions below? Write in your exercise book. Then listen to your CD and check your answers.*

***a)*** *Dana is at JFK airport in New York. She wants a bus to the town centre.*

She asks someone politely...
- *if they know where the buses leave from.*
- where the buses stop in the town centre.
- how long the bus ride takes.
- how much bus tickets cost.
- where you buy the bus tickets.

Excuse me, *do you know where the buses leave from, please?*

***b)*** *Patrick is having an interview for a holiday job at a garage.*

He asks the boss ...
- *what he would have to do exactly.*
- what time the garage opens.
- if he would have to work on Saturdays.
- how many hours he would have to work a week.
- when he could start.

6322

*What would I have to do exactly?*

## 23 Describing a picture (Brainstorming vocabulary) ▸ SF (p. 135) · WB (pp. 72–73) 30

*When you describe a picture you usually have to ...*

- say where it is, e.g. *a scene in winter, a city street*, etc.
- say what is where: *in the background/foreground/middle; behind, next to*, etc.
- talk about the people (How many? What are they doing/wearing?).
- say how the people are probably feeling, what they are thinking.
- use adjectives to talk about the atmosphere: *happy, relaxed*, etc.

***a)*** *Look at the picture below and brainstorm your ideas for vocabulary. Write down words to describe the scene in your exercise book. If you don't know the words you need, use your dictionary.*

**Tip 17**

**Useful phrases for talking about pictures:**
*The picture shows a scene in summer/at a beach/in a big city/in the mountains...*
*It looks as if the people are ...*
*The woman/man on the right is laughing/chatting ...*
*Maybe she/he is thinking that ...*
*She might be ...*
*The people look happy/ excited ...*

**Tip 18**

**Answering questions**
Show that you can express[1] your opinion and can give reasons and arguments for it.
Here are some ideas:
*I can't ski so I think summer holidays are better.*
*In my opinion skiing holidays are too expensive.*
*I like holidays where I can ... I like swimming and I'd like to learn to snowboard too because ...*
*Sport plays an important role in my free time. I ... every week .*

***b)*** *Be prepared to answer general questions that have to do with the picture indirectly. Listen to the five questions on your CD (30). Answer each question with at least two complete sentences. You can make notes in your exercise book first. Then practise your answers, first from your notes, then without your notes. Concentrate on speaking clearly, but not too quickly.*

[1] express [ɪk'spres] *äußern, ausdrücken*

## 24 Comparing pictures ▸ SF (p. 135) • WB (pp. 72–73) 🎧 31

*When you compare two pictures, talk about the differences and compare the advantages and disadvantages.*

***a)*** *Think of words and phrases to talk about these pictures. Make two lists below.*

| A In a town | B In the country |
|---|---|
| lots of people, cars, shops | few people, |
| | |
| | |
| | |
| | |
| | |
| | |

***b)*** *Use your notes in a) to talk about the two pictures. You can record what you say.*

***c)*** *You often have to talk about pictures or a given topic with your exam partner. Your dialogue should be realistic, so ask relevant questions. Here are some questions that you could ask about the topic of this exercise. Ask these questions in English, then check them on your CD (🎧 31):*

1 Wohnst du in der Stadt oder auf dem Land?

2 Würdest du lieber irgendwo anders wohnen?

3 Wie kommst du in die Schule?

4 Wo wohnen deine Freunde?

5 Welche Vorteile hat man auf dem Land?

6 Welche Vorteile hat man in der Stadt?

7 Wenn du nicht in Deutschland wohntest, wo würdest du wohnen wollen?

***d)*** **Extra** *Ask your partner the questions 2–7 in c) in English.*

### Tip 19

**General advice**
- You don't have to speak quickly, but you must speak clearly.
- Don't answer questions with *yes* or *no* only.
- If you repeat an idea or opinion, say it differently.
- Say what you want, even if you think the examiner may not agree.

### Tip 20

If you don't understand what the examiner/interviewer says, it's good to know some useful, polite **phrases** by heart:
*Could you repeat that, please?*
*Could you explain that again/once more, please?*
*Sorry, I can't quite follow you.*
*Do you mean that I have to ...?*
*Sorry, what exactly do I have to do?*
*Sorry, but I didn't quite understand/catch what you said.*

### Tip 21

**Useful partner questions**
When you have to talk to your exam partner, exchange information, give opinions, express feelings. You could start like this:
*In my opinion, ...*
*I have read that ...*
*What do you think about ...?*
*Don't you think that ...?*
*Do you agree that ...?*
*Isn't it better to ... than to ...?*
*What's your opinion about ...?*

## 25 London travel (Mediating a written text) ▸ WB (pp. 74, 76)

**a)** *You are going to visit London with your family and you want to tell them the best way to travel around the city. You find this information. Mark the main facts first. Then make notes below in German.*

**Tip 22**

Mark the **main facts** and summarize them. Leave out unimportant details. Don't translate.

### London Travelcards for international visitors

If you are planning to travel in and around London, it's best to buy a Travelcard. You will save money and you will have complete freedom[1] of travel on the Tube, buses, trams, Docklands Light Railway (DLR) and most local trains across the whole of London. You can even get riverboat tickets one third cheaper.

There are many different kinds of Travelcards. You have to choose whatever is best for you. You can buy a Travelcard for just one day, three days, seven days or even longer. London is divided into 6 travel zones and Travelcards cover different zones. Zones 1 and 2 cover Central London and most of the famous London sights. Zone 6 takes you to the outer areas of the city, e.g. Heathrow Airport. You must decide which zones you want to visit.

You must also know when you want to start your journey. If you plan to travel before 9.30 am (Mon–Fri), you will need a Peak Travelcard. If you travel after 9.30 am, you can buy an Off-Peak Travelcard, which is a little cheaper. For example, an Off-Peak One-day Travelcard for Zones 1 and 2 costs £5.60 for an adult (16 and over). By comparison, the Peak One-day Travelcard costs £7.20. There are special reduced prices for children (5–15). Children under 5 go free. You can buy your Travelcard online or all over the city at Tube stations and travel information centres.

(Prices: February 2010)

**Tip 23**

When you mediate written information, the order is not important. Before you start, find the **main points**. Sometimes it's easier to mark **key words** and note information under headings. Here: *advantages, travel zones, journey times, prices.*

**b)** *You tell your parents what you have found out, but they still have a few questions. Give short answers in German.*

1 Wo kann man die Travelcard kaufen? ____________

2 Kann man mit der Travelcard vom Flughafen in die Stadt fahren? ____________

3 Du bist 16 und Schüler. Musst du schon den vollen Preis bezahlen? ____________

4 Müssen wir für Tommy zahlen? Er ist ja erst vier. ____________

[1] freedom ['fri:dəm] *Freiheit*

## 26 What did he say? (Mediating what you hear) ▸ *WB (pp. 74, 76)* 32

*Explain what you hear to your American exchange student. Listen to the radio programme and make a few notes while you are listening. Use your own words and tell him the main things in a few sentences.*

Yes, he's talking about the 'Night Flyers'. They

## 27 Explaining signs (Using modal auxiliaries)

*You are in town with your dog, your bike and your British cousin. How can you explain these German signs to her? Tick the correct answers.*

**Tip 24**

**Be careful!**
*you can't ...*
*du kannst/darfst nicht ...*
*you have to .../you must*
*du musst ...*
*you don't have to .../you needn't ...*
*du musst/brauchst nicht ...*
*you mustn't ...*
*du darfst nicht ...*

**1**

WIR MÜSSEN DRAUSSEN BLEIBEN

- [x] We can't take the dog in there.
- [ ] Dogs are allowed inside.
- [x] Dogs have to stay outside.

**2** PARKEN VERBOTEN
Bitte keine Fahrräder abstellen!

- [ ] You can't leave your bike here.
- [ ] You mustn't leave your bike here.
- [ ] You aren't allowed to leave your bike here.

**3** Ganztägig geöffnet
Tischreservierung nicht erforderlich

- [ ] You needn't book[1] a table.
- [ ] You should book a table.
- [ ] You don't have to book a table.

**4** KONZERTKARTEN
Bitte anstellen

- [ ] You can buy concert tickets here.
- [ ] You have to stand in line.

**5** Betreten des Turms
AUF EIGENE GEFAHR

- [ ] You mustn't go up the tower.
- [ ] You can go up the tower but at your own risk[2].
- [ ] You shouldn't really go up the tower.

**6** RUHEZONE! BITTE
MOBILTELEFONE AUSSCHALTEN!

- [ ] You have to be quiet.
- [ ] You aren't allowed to use your mobile.
- [ ] You needn't turn off your mobile.

**7** STADTBIBLIOTHEK
Haupteingang wegen Renovierungsarbeiten geschlossen. Bitte Nebeneingang links um die Ecke benutzen.

- [ ] We can't use the main entrance[3].
- [ ] We have to use the side entrance.

6627

[1] book [bʊk] *buchen* [2] risk *Risiko* [3] main entrance ['meɪn 'entrəns] *Haupteingang*

## 28 Christmas on the beach (Simple present and present progressive) ▸ GF (p. 159)

*Complete the text with the correct form: simple present (e.g. she goes) or present progressive (e.g. she is going).*

This year Mike from Bristol _is spending_ (spend) Christmas in Sydney with his Australian girlfriend, Maggie. Like hundreds of other young people, they ____________ (celebrate[1]) on Bondi Beach. At the moment they ____________ (swim) in the sea. Maggie ____________ (know) about the dangers of the ozone hole and how quickly the sun ____________ (burn) your skin, so she ____________ (~~lie~~) in the sun on the beach. And she never ____________ (go) on the beach at midday when it ____________ (get) really hot. But lots of British people, like Mike, ____________ (~~seem~~) to worry about that.

6728

**Tip 25**

The **simple present** is important in everyday communication: writing/talking about yourself and others, what you often do, like, think.
You also need it for writing:
- summaries of stories, film and book reviews
- descriptions of characters in fictional texts
- comments on opinions/ideas
- your personal statement on your CV.

**Tip 26**

Use the **present progressive** for actions and situations that are going on at the time.
Remember, some verbs are not used in the progressive form: *believe, belong, know, like, need, own, seem.*

**Tip 27**

Use the **simple past** for completed actions in the past, often with signal words – *yesterday, last year,* etc. Use it in stories or reports, or to talk about *when* something happened.
Make questions and negatives with '*did*'.
Use the **past progressive** for actions that were not completed at a time in the past.

## 29 He didn't understand (Simple past or past progressive) ▸ GF (p. 160)

*Complete with verbs in the simple past (e.g. went, liked) or past progressive (e.g. was/were reading). There are some negative and some question forms.*

Lina _wanted_ (want) to improve her English, so last year she ____________ (go) as an au pair to the USA. She didn't ____________ (not know) much about her American host family, but when she ____________ (arrive) in Atlanta, all five members of her host family[2] ____________ (wait) at the airport to meet her. While Lina ____________ (chat) to Mrs Jackson about the flight, Mr Jackson ____________ (pick) up her large bag, but Lina ____________ (say) loudly, 'Oh, no, Mr Jackson. You mustn't carry[3] my bag.' So Mr Jackson ____________ (put) the bag down again. He ____________ (look) puzzled and embarrassed because he ____________ (~~understand~~). Why ____________ (Lina, want) to carry the big bag herself? ____________ (she, have) something important in her bag, or something that might break? Mr Jackson ____________ (~~say~~) anything. When they ____________ (walk) out of the airport, Lina ____________ (think), 'Why ____________ (he, put) my bag down? Is it too heavy[4] for him? What's the problem?' Do you know?

6729

[1] celebrate ['selɪbreɪt] *feiern* [2] host family [həʊst] *Gastfamilie* [3] carry ['kæri] *tragen* [4] heavy ['hevi] *schwer*

## 30 Saying it differently (Changing sentence structure)

*You often have to say something differently without changing the meaning. Use the word in brackets to express the meaning in a different way.*

**Tip 28**

It is important to say something **differently** when you:
- write a summary.
- mediate what someone says.
- answer questions about a text.
- take notes from a written text.

1 The phone rang while Mel was watching her favourite soap. (during)

The phone rang during Mel's favourite soap.

2 It was her boyfriend. The last time she had seen him was three days ago. (for)

She hadn't ______________________

3 'Come to see the new film at the Majestic with me,' he said. (wanted)

He ______________________ to see the new film at the Majestic with him.

4 There was a long queue at the cinema, so they had to wait. (because)

They had to ______________________

5 The film wasn't as bad as the last one they had seen. (better)

The film was ______________________

## 31 The flying doctors of Australia (RFDS) (Using linking words) ▸ WB (p. 74)

*Join two sentences with the linking word in brackets. Change the order of the sentences only where necessary.*

1 About 10% of Australians live far away from towns and cities.
They can't get medical help easily. (so)

About 10% of Australians live far away from towns and cities, so they can't get medical help easily.

2 Before the RFDS started, many people died. Doctors could not reach[1] them. (because)

______________________

3 The Service is very well organized. It can reach people in over 80% of the country. (so)

______________________

4 The RFDS has opened more than 20 bases all over the country. Doctors can reach people quickly. (so that)

______________________

______________________

5 It is not easy to pass the tests and interviews. Lots of young people want to go to the RFDS. (although)

______________________

6 The RFDS was started in about 1930. The RFDS is a 24-hour service. (which)

______________________

6831

[1] reach [ri:tʃ] *erreichen*

## 32 Explaining words (Paraphrasing) ▸ *WB (p. 74)*

*If you don't know the English word for what you want to say, you can paraphrase it. Here are some helpful phrases:*

It's someone who … • It's something that … • It's something you use to … • It's a/the place where … It's like … • It's a/the …

*You are talking to your American exchange student about job adverts in a local newspaper. Explain these words in English:*

*1* Stellenanzeige: It's a notice in a newspaper that tells people about jobs.

*2* Aushilfe: ______

*3* Dom: ______

*4* Führerschein: ______

*5* Rezeption: ______

6932 *6* Bezahlung: ______

## 33 Making texts more interesting (Using adjectives)

***a)*** *Choose adjectives from the box that you could use with the words in 1–4 below. Some adjectives fit into more than one list. Then add at least three more suitable adjectives to each list.*

| boring • busy • clean • excited • exciting • healthy • interesting • noisy • polite • quiet • relaxing • serious |
|---|

*1* a job: ______

*2* a town/city: ______

*3* the countryside: ______

*4* a job candidate[1]: ______

***b)*** *Write one or two sentences each with the words in a). Use as many adjectives as you can from each list.*

*1* I would like to have a job that's interesting and useful

______

*2* ______

______

*3* ______

______

*4* ______

______

[1] candidate ['kændidət] *Kandidat/in, Bewerber/in*

## 34 About Simon (Word order in subordinate clauses)

*Put the words in the boxes in the correct order to make subordinate clauses.*

1 [Since] [school] [Simon] [left], he has worked as a shop assistant in a supermarket.

Since Simon left school, ...

2 Simon likes his work because [a lot of new things] [learn] [can] [he].

... ______

3 Simon plays football for the local team, so [has to] [he] [train] [twice a week].

... ______

4 If [well] [he] [works], the manager lets him go home earlier.

______

5 That's usually on the days when [has to] [he] [football training] [go to].

... ______

6 The manager lets him go early because [of the local team] [he] [too] [is] [a big supporter].

... ______

**Tip 29**

Word order in English is different from German. It is always **Subject-Verb-Object**. Compare:
*Since S.* ***left*** *school he has…*
*Seitdem S. die Schule* ***verließ****, hat er…*

## 35 A trip to New York (Correcting your text) ▸ *WB (p. 75)*

*Here is Ella's e-mail to her online friend in Washington. Correct the mistakes.*

Hi Kelly!
Here we are in New York! It's so cool here. I really enjoyed ~~planing~~ our sightseeing tour ~~befor~~ we came and we've done ~~the most~~ of the things on my list. We've been in New York ~~since~~ two days. The ~~whether~~ was great yesterday, so we ~~have gone~~ up the Empire State Building. I ~~made~~ some pretty cool photos and I ~~heared~~ so ~~many informations over~~ the building. It was very ~~intresting~~. I have to talk English because my parents ~~want that I~~ ask a lot of questions about where ~~we must go~~ and what ~~we could do~~. The ~~american peoples~~ are very friendly and ~~helpfull~~. They always ~~say~~ me what I want to know. New York isn't so far from Washington. Maybe I could ~~travell~~ down to Washington ~~with the~~ train to see you for a day or two. Would that be OK? ~~I'm calling~~ you this evening. ~~Than~~ you can tell me what you ~~mean~~. If I ~~would come~~ to visit you, I'm sure we ~~had~~ lots of fun!
Ella

Correct

planning,

______

______

______

______

7035

## LISTENING SKILLS ▸ *p. 141*

### SF REVISION Listening

#### Was muss ich allgemein beim *Listening* beachten?

**Vor dem Hören:**

- Überlege, worum es in dem Hörtext gehen wird. Frag dich, was du schon über das Thema weißt.
- Lies die Aufgabe gut durch, damit du weißt, worauf du achten sollst: auf die Hauptgedanken oder auf bestimmte Informationen, wie z.B. Namen, Uhrzeit, Jahreszahlen.
- Bereite dich darauf vor, Notizen zu machen. Leg z.B. eine Tabelle oder Liste an.

**Beim Hören:**

- Du musst nicht alles verstehen. Konzentriere dich auf das Wesentliche. Oft werden wichtige Informationen wiederholt.
- Achte auf Geräusche und unterschiedliche Stimmen. Was ein Sprecher/eine Sprecherin besonders betont, das ist wichtig!
- Wenn du gezielt nach Informationen suchst, denk an die Aufgabe und lass dich von anderen Einzelheiten nicht ablenken. Die Informationen, die du suchst, kommen vielleicht in einer anderen Reihenfolge vor, als du sie erwartest.
- Manche Signalwörter machen es dir leichter, den Hörtext zu verstehen:
  - Aufzählung: **and**, **another**, **too**
  - Gegensatz: **although**, **but**
  - Grund, Folge: **because, so**, **so that**
  - Vergleich: **larger/older/... than**, **more**, **most**
  - Reihenfolge: **before**, **after**, **then**, **next**, **later**, **when**, **at last**, **at the same time**
- Mach nur kurze Notizen, z.B. Anfangsbuchstaben, Symbole oder Stichworte, schreib keine ganzen Sätze. Unterteile Telefonnummern beim Aufschreiben: 0171 572 42 589.

**Nach dem Hören:**

- Vervollständige deine Notizen sofort.
- Konzentriere dich beim zweiten Hören auf das, was du zuerst nicht gut verstanden hast.

#### Worauf sollte ich bei automatischen Telefonansagen achten?

Wenn du eine telefonische Auskunft einholen willst, hörst du manchmal eine automatische Telefonansage.

- Keine Panik! Du kannst eine automatische Telefonansage mehrmals hören.
- Achte besonders auf Zahlen! Meist wirst du aufgefordert, bestimmte Tasten auf deinem Telefon zu drücken, um die gewünschte Information zu erhalten. Oft werden diese Zahlen wiederholt.
- Überlege dir vorher, welche Informationen du suchst und auf welche Schlüsselwörter du dafür achten solltest. Schreib sie auf.
- Höre dann besonders genau zu, wenn deine Schlüsselwörter genannt werden und mach dir Notizen zu ihnen.

---

## REVISION READING COURSE – Zusammenfassung ▸ *pp. 144–145*

### Working out the meaning of words

#### Was hilft dir, unbekannte Wörter zu verstehen?

1. **Bilder** zeigen oft die Dinge, die du im Text nicht verstehst. Wenn es Bilder zum Text gibt, dann schau sie dir vor dem Lesen genau an.
2. Oft hilft dir der **Textzusammenhang**, z.B. *When we **reached** the station, Judy went to the ticket machine to buy our tickets.*
3. Manche englischen Wörter werden **ähnlich wie im Deutschen** geschrieben oder ausgesprochen, z.B. **excellent**, **millionaire**, **nation**, **reality**.
4. Manchmal stecken in unbekannten Wörtern **bekannte Teile**, z.B. **friendliness**, **helpless**, **understandable**, **gardener**, **tea bag**, **waiting room**.

### Skimming and Scanning

Beim **Skimming** überfliegst du einen Text schnell, um dir einen ersten **Überblick** zu verschaffen, worum es geht. Du willst herausfinden, ob ein Text, den du im Internet oder in einem Buch gefunden hast, überhaupt nützliche Informationen zu deinem Thema (z.B. für ein Referat) enthält. Achte beim Skimming auf:

- die **Überschrift**,
- die **Zwischenüberschriften** und **hervorgehobene** Wörter oder Sätze,
- die **Bilder** und **Bildunterschriften**,
- den **ersten** und **letzten Satz** jedes Absatzes,
- **Grafiken**, **Statistiken** und die **Quelle** des Textes.

Beim **Scanning** suchst du in einem Text nach **bestimmten Informationen**, die z.B. für ein Referat wichtig sind. Dazu brauchst du nicht den gesamten Text zu lesen, sondern du suchst nach Schlüsselwörtern (**key words**) und liest nur dort genauer, wo du sie findest. Geh dabei so vor:

**Schritt 1:** Denk an das Schlüsselwort, nach dem du suchst, oder schreib es auf.

**Schritt 2:** Geh mit den Augen und dem Finger schnell durch den Text, in breiten Schlingen wie bei einem „S" oder „Z" oder von oben nach unten wie bei einem „U". Dabei hast du das Schriftbild oder das Bild des Wortes, nach dem du suchst, vor Augen. Das gesuchte Wort wird dir sofort „ins Auge springen". Lies nur dort weiter, um Näheres zu erfahren.

**Schritt 3:** Wenn das Schlüsselwort, nach dem du suchst, im Text nicht vorkommt, überleg dir, welche anderen Wörter mit den benötigten Informationen zu tun haben, und such nach diesen.

### Finding the main ideas of a text

#### Wie finde ich die Hauptaussagen eines Textes?

1. Jeder Text dreht sich um ein Thema oder hat eine Hauptaussage, z.B. *This summer we have been raising money for the Hickery Soup Kitchen.* Diese Hauptaussage findest du oft im **ersten Absatz**. Lies ihn deshalb besonders gründlich durch.
2. Die Hauptaussage wird in der Regel durch weitere Aussagen bzw. Gedanken unterstützt, z.B. *To raise money we have mainly been to two churches.* Du findest sie oft im ersten oder letzten Satz der nachfolgenden Absätze.
3. Diese weiteren Aussagen bzw. Gedanken werden meist durch Beispiele und Begründungen ergänzt, z.B. *Lots of people have given money ... Altogether we've raised $427.*

**Tipp**

Die folgenden Wörter oder Wendungen werden oft im Zusammenhang mit Begründungen oder Beispielen verwendet:
and so • because • e.g. / for example • etc. • for lots of reasons • this shows that • that's why • ... % of ... are ...

### Drawing conclusions

#### Wie funktioniert schlussfolgerndes Lesen?

1. Die einfachste Form des schlussfolgernden Lesens besteht darin, die Informationen aus verschiedenen Textstellen zusammenzuführen. Beim Text auf S.17 im Schülerbuch z.B. sollst du beschreiben, wie Zita Wallace gestohlen wurde. Dazu musst du dir mehrere Textstellen ansehen.
2. Manchmal steht die Antwort auf eine Frage nicht direkt im Text. Dann musst du sie dir erschließen. Du fragst dich z.B., ob die Kinder der „stolen generations" lange auf eine Entschuldigung der australischen Regierung warten mussten. Dafür musst du Fakten im Text finden, die etwas mit der Frage zu tun haben:
   FACTS: – the policy (of stealing children) ended after 60 years in 1970 – Australian government apologized in 2008.
   CONCLUSION: the Australian government apologized 38 years later – that's a very long time

---

## SPEAKING AND WRITING SKILLS ▸ *pp. 146–148*

## SPEAKING COURSE – Zusammenfassung

### Having a conversation

#### Ein Gespräch beginnen

Es gibt immer mehrere Möglichkeiten:

– **wenn du etwas erfragen willst** *(z.B. den Weg oder die Uhrzeit)*: Excuse me, do you know ... • Excuse me, can you tell me ...
– **wenn du jemanden begrüßen möchtest oder kennen lernst:** Hi • Hello oder Good morning • Good evening (bei Erwachsenen) ... Oft kann man das Gespräch dann mit einer allgemeinen Bemerkung weiterführen: Great day today! • That's a great ...
– **wenn du jemanden wieder triffst:** Hi, how are you doing? Hi, ..., how are things?

**Tipp**

- Oft hört man zur Begrüßung auch How are you? oder How do you do? Das sind einfache Begrüßungsformeln. Es wird nicht erwartet, dass man darauf eine Antwort gibt.
- Am besten sagst du einfach Fine, thanks. How about you?

### Ein Gespräch führen

Für den weiteren Verlauf des Gesprächs sind diese Wendungen nützlich:
- **sich vorstellen:** By the way, my name's ... • I'm ... • Nice to meet you.
- **Smalltalk machen:** Have you ... before? • Have you ever ...? • Where are you from? • Do you like ...? • What about you?
- **um Hilfe bitten und anderen helfen:** Do you know where ...? • Can you tell me ...? • Sure, no problem • Why don't you ...?
- **sich verabschieden:** See you tomorrow/next week. • Bye!

Und wenn du etwas nicht verstanden hast, kannst du immer nachfragen:
Sorry, I didn't get that. • Sorry, can you say that again, please?

## Taking part in a job interview

### Sich vorbereiten

Auf ein Vorstellungsgespräch musst du dich unbedingt vorbereiten. Du solltest Fragen zu den folgenden Bereichen beantworten können:
- deine Eigenschaften (**personal qualities**), Stärken (**strengths**) und Schwächen (**weaknesses**),
- deine Interessen (**interests**) und Arbeitserfahrungen (**work experience**),
- was dich an dem Jobangebot reizt (**why you're interested in the job**).

Überleg dir auch eigene Fragen, zum Beispiel zu deinem Tätigkeitsbereich (**What kind of tasks would I have to do?**) oder zur Bezahlung (**What is the pay?**).

### Im Vorstellungsgespräch

Im Vorstellungsgespräch ist es wichtig, dass du freundlich bist und dich als positiver und interessierter Mensch präsentierst:
- **bei der Begrüßung:** Hello, nice to meet you. / Good morning ...
- **warum du dich bewirbst:** I'm really interested in / I'm good at ..., so I think ...
- **wenn es um deine Joberfahrungen geht:** I really enjoyed working with ...
- **bei der Verabschiedung:** Goodbye and thank you very much.

**Tipp**
- Hör gut zu, wenn du etwas gefragt wirst.
- Sprich nicht zu viel, aber auch nicht zu wenig.
- Sprich nicht zu schnell.

## Having a discussion

### Seine Meinung zum Ausdruck bringen und erklären

1. **Expressing an opinion:** In einer Diskussion ist es gut, wenn du möglichst klar und deutlich sagst, was du zu einer bestimmten Frage denkst: I think ... • I feel ... • In my opinion ...
2. **Giving reasons and examples:** Genauso wichtig ist es, dass du Beispiele und Argumente nennst, die deine Meinung unterstützen: because ... • First ... / Second ... / And finally... • For example ... • Let me explain ... • That's why ... ?

### Auf andere in einer Diskussion reagieren

1. **Asking for clarification:** Manchmal ist es notwendig nachzuhaken, weil man ein Argument nicht verstanden hat: Could you say that again? • Sorry, but I don't understand what you mean.
2. **Agreeing with someone:** Wenn du die Meinung eines anderen unterstützen willst, kannst du das so zum Ausdruck bringen: I agree (with you/...) • That's a good point. • You're right.
3. **Disagreeing with someone:** Oft widerspricht man nicht direkt, sondern leitet seine Reaktion mit Sorry, ... oder I don't think ... ein. Zeig immer Respekt für die Meinung des oder der anderen. I don' t think you can say ... • I see what you mean but ... • Sorry, but that's not right. • Sorry, I don't agree with you • Yes, but ...

## Giving a presentation

### Useful phrases

**Einleitung:** Nenne am Beginn deines Vortrags dein Thema und gib einen kurzen Überblick darüber, worum es in deinem Vortrag geht: The topic of my talk today is ... • I'm going to divide this talk into four sections. • First, I'll give you some general facts about ... • Next I'll look at ... • Finally I'll ...
**Während der Präsentation:** Mach deutlich, wenn du einen neuen Abschnitt in deinem Vortrag beginnst:
Now please have a look at ... • On the next slide ... • Now I'd like to draw your attention to ... • As you can see in ...
**Schluss:** Am Ende deines Vortrags fass die wichtigsten Punkte zusammen. Frag deine Zuhörer, ob sie etwas nachfragen oder kommentieren möchten: To sum up my talk I ... • Please feel free to ask questions or comment on anything I've said.

## SF REVISION Paraphrasing

### Worum geht es beim Paraphrasing?

Paraphrasing bedeutet, etwas mit anderen Worten zu erklären. Das ist hilfreich, wenn dir ein bestimmtes Wort nicht einfällt oder wenn dein Gegenüber dich nicht verstanden hat (siehe auch ▸ *Mediation, S. 76*).

### Wie gehe ich beim Paraphrasing vor?

- Man kann mit einem Wort umschreiben, das dieselbe Bedeutung hat: To train is the same as to practise. Oder man sagt das Gegenteil: Alive is the opposite of dead.
- Manchmal braucht man mehrere Wörter, z. B. wenn man etwas beschreibt oder erklärt. Dabei benutzt man ein allgemeines Wort (**general word**) und nennt weitere Eigenschaften: A racing car is a very fast car.
- Oder du umschreibst das Wort mit **... is/are like ...**: A chef is like a cook, he or she is the main cook in a restaurant.
- Du kannst auch einen Relativsatz (**relative clause**) verwenden: A garage is the place where cars are checked and repaired.

## SF REVISION Brainstorming

### Wie gehe ich beim Brainstorming vor?

**Schritt 1:** Schreib alle Ideen so auf, wie sie dir einfallen. Es ist zunächst völlig egal, ob sie gut sind oder nicht. Du kannst die Ideen durcheinander auf einen Zettel schreiben oder schon etwas geordnet, z. B. für jede eine neue Zeile.

**Schritt 2:** Lies alle deine Ideen durch und wähle die besten aus. Dann sortiere sie und fasse sie sinnvoll zusammen. Dabei kannst du folgende **Techniken** anwenden:

1. Leg eine **Mindmap** an. Schreib das Thema in die Mitte eines Blattes Papier. Überlege, welche Oberbegriffe zu deiner Sammlung von Ideen passen. Verwende unterschiedliche Farben. Ergänze jede Idee, die zu einem Oberbegriff passt, auf einem Nebenast. Nimm dafür nur wichtige Schlüsselwörter. Du kannst statt Wörtern auch Symbole verwenden und Bilder ergänzen.
2. **The 5 Ws**: Schreib die **5** W-Fragen Who? What? Where? When? Why? in eine Tabelle. Die Ideen, die dir zu jeder Frage kommen, kannst du darunter schreiben.

---

## REVISION Writing course – Zusammenfassung ▸ *pp. 150–151*

**The steps of writing**

1. Brainstorming – Ideen sammeln, dann sortieren.
2. Schreiben. Dabei achte darauf,
   - deine Sätze zu verbinden und auszubauen (*Writing better sentences*),
   - deinen Text gut zu strukturieren (*Using paragraphs*),
   - bei einem Bericht die 5 Ws abzudecken (*Writing a report*).
3. Deinen Text inhaltlich und sprachlich überprüfen (*Correcting your text*).

### Writing better sentences

#### Linking words

Eine Geschichte klingt interessanter, wenn du die Sätze mit **linking words** miteinander verbindest, z. B.:

- **Time phrases** wie at 7 o'clock, every morning, a few minutes later, then, next ...
- **Konjunktionen** wie although, because, but, so ... that, that, when, while ...
- **Relativpronomen** wie that und who.

#### Adjektive und Adverbien

- Mit Adjektiven kannst du Personen, Orte oder Erlebnisse genauer und interessanter beschreiben. Vergleiche: The man looked into the house. ▸ The young man looked into the empty house.
- Mit Adverbien kannst du beschreiben, **wie** jemand etwas macht: The young man looked nervously into the empty house.

## Using paragraphs

### Structuring a text

Ein längerer Text ist besser zu verstehen, wenn er in mehrere Absätze unterteilt ist:
- eine Einleitung (**beginning**) – hier schreibst du, worum es geht,
- einen Hauptteil (**middle**) – hier schreibst du mehr über dein Thema,
- einen Schluss (**end**) – hier bringst du den Text zu einem interessanten Ende.

### Topic sentences

Am Anfang eines Absatzes sind kurze, einleitende Sätze (**topic sentences**) gut, weil sie den Lesern sofort sagen, worum es geht, z.B.:

1. Orte: My trip to ... was fantastic. / ... is famous for ... / ... is a great place.
2. Personen: ... is great/funny/interesting/clever ...
3. Aktivitäten: ... is great fun. / Lots of people ... every day.

### Wie kann ich meine Absätze interessant gestalten?

- Beginne mit einem interessanten Einstiegssatz: You'll never guess what happened to me today! / Did I tell you that ...?
- Fang für jeden neuen Aspekt einen neuen Absatz an.
- Beende deinen Text mit einer Zusammenfassung oder etwas Persönlichem.

## Writing a report – collecting and organizing ideas

### Worauf kommt es bei einem Bericht an?

- Gib dem Leser **eine schnelle Orientierung**, was passiert ist.
- Beginne mit **wichtigen Informationen** und gib erst dann Detailinformationen.
- Ein Bericht gibt immer Antworten auf die **5 Ws**: Who? What? When? Where? Why? und manchmal auch auf How?
- Verwende das **simple past**.

## Correcting your text

Ein Text ist noch nicht „fertig", wenn du ihn zu Ende geschrieben hast. Du solltest ihn immer mehr als einmal durchlesen:
- einmal, um zu sehen, ob er vollständig und gut verständlich ist,
- noch einmal, um ihn auf Fehler zu überprüfen, z.B. Rechtschreibfehler oder Grammatikfehler (s.u.).

### Spelling mistakes

Lies deinen Text langsam, Wort für Wort. Wenn du unsicher bist, hilft dir ein Wörterbuch. Beachte folgende Regeln:

**Tipp**
- Manche Wörter haben Buchstaben, die man nicht spricht, aber schreibt, z.B. knife, climb.
- Manchmal ändert sich die Schreibweise, wenn ein Wort eine Endung erhält, z.B. take ▸ taking, terrible ▸ terribly, lucky ▸ luckily, try ▸ tries (**aber** stay ▸ stays), run ▸ running, drop ▸ dropped.
- Beim Plural tritt manchmal noch ein -e zum -s, z.B. church ▸ churches.

tomato [tə'mɑːtəʊ], *pl* **tomatoes** Tomate II

wife [waɪf], *pl* **wives** [waɪvz] Ehefrau II

drop (-**pp**-) [drɒp] fallen lassen I

forget (-**tt**-) [fə'get] vergessen I

### Grammar mistakes

Diese Tipps helfen dir, typische Fehler zu vermeiden:

**Tipp**
- Im **simple present** wird in der 3. Person Singular -s angehängt: she knows
- **Unregelmäßige Verben:** Manche Verben bilden die Formen des *simple past* und des Partizip Perfekt *(past participle)* unregelmäßig, z.B. go – went – gone; buy – bought – bought. Die unregelmäßigen Formen musst du lernen.
- **Verneinung bei Vollverben:** Im *simple present* mit *don't/doesn't*, im *simple past* mit didn't, z.B. He doesn't speak French, he didn't learn it at school.
- **Satzstellung**: Im Englischen gilt immer (auch im Nebensatz):
  a) subject – verb – object (SVO): ... when I saw my brother.
  ... als ich meinen Bruder sah.
  b) Orts- vor Zeitangabe: I bought a nice book in the city yesterday.

## MEDIATION SKILLS ▶ *p. 155*

### SF REVISION Mediation

#### Worauf muss ich bei *mediation* achten?

- Übersetze nicht alles wörtlich.
- Gib nur das Wesentliche weiter, lass Unwichtiges weg.
- Verwende kurze und einfache Sätze.
- Wenn du ein Wort nicht kennst, umschreibe es oder ersetze es durch ein anderes Wort.

#### Was kann ich tun, wenn ich ein wichtiges Wort nicht kenne?

Vielleicht findest du es manchmal schwer, mündliche Aussagen oder schriftliche Textvorlagen in die andere Sprache zu übertragen, z. B. weil:

- dein Wortschatz nicht ausreicht,
- dir bekannte Wörter „im Stress“ nicht einfallen,
- spezielle Fachbegriffe auftauchen.

Manche Wörter kannst du umschreiben, z. B. mithilfe von Relativsätzen wie:

It's somebody/a person who ...
It's something that you use to ...
It's an animal that ...
It's a place where ...

Schau dir auch den Abschnitt zu Paraphrasing an (*S. 74*).

---

## Unit 1

### GF 4 Indirect speech (I) ▶ *p. 163*

| | | |
|---|---|---|
| **Indirect speech** (reporting verb: simple present) | Zita Wallace says **that** she **saw** terrible things and **that** she **will** never **forget** those first hours. | ◂ In der **indirekten Rede** (*indirect* oder *reported speech*) wird berichtet, was jemand sagt oder gesagt hat. Die indirekte Rede wird mit Verben wie *say, tell sb., add, answer, explain, write* eingeleitet. |
| **Indirect speech** (reporting verb: simple past) | Zita Wallace said **that** she had seen terrible things. She added **that** she would never forget those first hours. | ◂ Wenn das **einleitende Verb im *simple past*** steht (*she said/told us/explained/answered* usw.), dann werden die Zeitformen der direkten Rede meist verändert: Sie werden um eine Zeitstufe in die Vergangenheit „zurückverschoben“ *(backshift of tenses)*. |

**Veränderungen der Zeitformen bei einleitendem Verb im *simple past***

| | Direct speech | Indirect speech |
|---|---|---|
| **present ▸ past** | 'I don't care about money.'<br>'I'm waiting for an apology.' | She **said** she didn't care about money.<br>She **said** she was waiting for an apology. |
| **past ▸ past perfect** | 'I saw terrible things.' | She **told** us she had seen terrible things. |
| ***can* ▸ *could*** | 'You can go shopping with us.' | The nuns **said** that the girls could go shopping with them. |
| ***will*-future ▸ *would* + infinitive** | 'I'll never forget those days.' | She **said** she would never forget those days. |
| ***going to*-future ▸ *was/were going to* + infinitive** | 'The government is going to apologize.' | They **said** the government was going to apologize. |
| **present perfect ▸ past perfect** | 'I haven't forgotten that evening.' | She **added** that she hadn't forgotten that evening. |

Verben im *past perfect* bleiben unverändert, da man sie nicht weiter „zurückverschieben“ kann.

## Unit 2

## GF 5 Indirect speech (II) ▸ p. 164

### 5.1 Commands and requests

*Simon* Look for clothes for the interview. And don't be shy.
Simon told them to look for clothes for the interview. And he told them not to be shy.

◂ **Aufforderungen, Anordnungen** und **Ratschläge** werden in der indirekten Rede meist mit ***tell sb. to do sth.*** (bzw. ***tell sb. not to do sth.***) wiedergegeben.

*Simon* Mani, please choose a new tie.
Simon asked Mani to choose a new tie.

◂ Eine **Bitte** wird meist mit ***ask sb. to do sth.*** (bzw. ***ask sb. not to do sth.***) wiedergegeben.

### 5.2 Questions

Auch bei Fragen in der indirekten Rede werden die Zeitformen in die Vergangenheit „zurückverschoben", wenn das einleitende Verb im *simple past* steht.

**Direct question** (with question word): What do you know about my business?
**Indirect question**: Rita asked Mani **what** he knew about her business.

◂ Wenn die direkte **Frage mit einem Fragewort** beginnt (*what, when, where, why, how* usw.), dann wird das Fragewort in der indirekten Frage beibehalten.

**Direct question** (yes/no question): Do you have any weaknesses?
**Indirect question**: Rita asked him **if** he had any weaknesses.

◂ Handelt es sich bei der direkten Frage um eine **Frage ohne Fragewort** *(yes/no question)*, dann wird die indirekte Frage mit ***if*** („ob") eingeleitet.

## Unit 3

## GF 6 Participles ▸ p. 165

### 6.1 REVISION Participle forms

**Present participle** *(-ing)*:

play → **playing** try → **trying**
phone → **phoning** plan → **planning**

◂ Das **Partizip Präsens** *(present participle)* bildet man durch Anhängen von ***-ing*** an den Infinitiv.
Beachte die Besonderheiten bei der Schreibung.

**Past participle, regular verbs** *(-ed)*:

play → **played** try → **tried**
phone → **phoned** plan → **planned**

◂ Das **Partizip Perfekt** *(past participle)* eines regelmäßigen Verbs wird durch Anhängen von ***-ed*** an den Infinitiv gebildet. Beachte auch hier die Besonderheiten bei der Schreibung.

**Past participle, irregular verbs:**

go → **gone** make → **made**
take → **taken** write → **written**

Bedenke, dass unregelmäßige Verben eigene 3. Formen haben, die man einzeln lernen muss.

**Additional information**

### 6.2 Participle clauses instead of relative clauses

Partizipialsätze können Relativsätze ersetzen.

1 He saw other kids **having fun outside.**
... andere Jugendliche, die sich draußen amüsierten.

2 Shane is a reliable young man **looking for his first job.**
... junger Mann, der seine erste Anstellung sucht.

◂ Partizipialsätze mit ***present participle*** (Sätze **1** und **2**) entsprechen Relativsätzen im **Aktiv**:
**1** ... ***having*** *fun* = ... ***who were having*** *fun*
**2** ... ***looking*** *for his first job* = ... ***who is looking*** *for ...*

3 He saw the posters **stuck up in town.**
... die Poster, die in der Stadt aufgehängt waren.

◂ Partizipialsätze mit ***past participle*** (Satz **3**) entsprechen Relativsätzen im **Passiv**:
**3** ... ***stuck*** *up in town* = ... ***that were stuck up*** ...

## GF 7 The passive ▸ *p. 166*

### 7.2 Form

Das Passiv bildet man mit einer **Form von *be*** und der 3. Form des Verbs (Partizip Perfekt, *past participle*).

**The passive**

| | |
|---|---|
| **Simple present:** | So much trash is thrown into the springs. |
| ***am/are/is*** + past participle | So viel Müll wird in die Quellen geworfen. |
| **Simple past:** | I was beaten by my best friend. |
| ***was/were*** + past participle | Ich wurde von meinem besten Freund besiegt. |
| **Present perfect:** | A lot of coins and bills have been collected. |
| ***have/has been*** + past participle | Eine Menge Münzen und Noten sind gesammelt worden. |
| ***will*-future:** | The food will be given to the Soup Kitchen tomorrow. |
| ***will be*** + past participle | Morgen werden die Lebensmittel der Suppenküche übergeben (werden). |
| **Modal auxiliaries:** | The food can be stored there overnight. |
| ***can/must/should/... be*** | Die Lebensmittel können dort über Nacht gelagert werden. |
| + past participle | Something must be done / should be done to help people in need. |
| | Es muss / sollte etwas getan werden, ... |

## Unit 4

## GF 8 Conditional sentences ▸ *p. 167*

### 8.1 REVISION Type 1 and type 2

If you run, you'll catch the bus.
Wenn du rennst, kriegst du den Bus noch.

If you miss the bus, you can take / should take / must take a taxi.
Wenn du den Bus verpasst, kannst/sollst/musst du ein Taxi nehmen.

| ***if*-Satz (Bedingung)** | **Hauptsatz (Folge)** |
|---|---|
| *If you run,* | *you'll catch the bus.* |
| *If you miss the bus,* | *you can take a taxi.* |
| ***simple present*** | **– *will-future*** |
| | **– *can/should/must* + Infinitiv** |

If you ran, you would catch the bus.
Wenn du rennen würdest, würdest du den Bus noch kriegen.
If you caught the bus, you could be home in time for dinner.
Wenn du den Bus kriegen würdest, könntest du rechtzeitig zum Abendessen daheim sein.

| ***if*-Satz (Bedingung)** | **Hauptsatz (Folge)** |
|---|---|
| *If you ran,* | *you would catch/could catch the bus.* |
| ***simple past*** | ***would/could* + Infinitiv** |

**Additional information**

### 8.2 Type 3

If you had run, you would have caught the bus.
Wenn du gerannt wärst, hättest du den Bus noch gekriegt.

If you had caught the bus, you could have had dinner with us.
Wenn du den Bus gekriegt hättest, hättest du mit uns Abendbrot essen können.

| ***if*-Satz (Bedingung)** | **Hauptsatz (Folge)** |
|---|---|
| *If you had run,* | *you would have caught/ could have caught the bus.* |
| ***past perfect*** | ***would/could* + *have* + Partizip Perfekt** |

**1 LISTENING Summer vacation**
*1* B; *2* B; *3* C; *4* C; *5* B; *6* B

**2 LISTENING A day in the life of …**
*a)* Why bushfires start
*b)* *1* F; *2* T; *3* F; *4* T; *5* F; *6* T; *7* T; *8* F; *9* T; *10* F

**3 READING Sydney for everyone**
*a)* Sydney's sights
*b)* Opening times, Sights information
*c)* *1* T; *2* F; *3* F; *4* N; *5* T; *6* F; *7* T; *8* F; *9* T; *10* F; *11* N; *12* T

**4a) WRITING An e-mail**
Hi/Dear …
Here I am in Sydney! It's a fantastic place! Today was a sightseeing day. First we went to see the famous Harbour Bridge. People were climbing it – crazy! After that we went to The Rocks, that's an interesting old area with colonial buildings, but with souvenir shops and cafés too.
We went to see the Opera House next – quite amazing, but we didn't have time for a tour. In the afternoon we did a boat trip round the harbour and we went under the Bridge. That was better than climbing it!
Tomorrow will be a Bondi Beach day, so we'll have to 'slip, slop, slap' because it's pretty hot here!
I'll write again tomorrow and tell you more news!
Love …

**4b) WRITING A summary**
The story is about Nina, her brother David and two friends who drive to Kakadu National Park to celebrate Nina's birthday. On the way they argue about the danger of saltwater crocodiles for tourists. David thinks they should be really careful because park rangers cannot guarantee visitor safety, but Nina says David is too scared. That evening they celebrate at the campsite and the next morning they leave for Jim Jim Falls. Nina and Mike want to go swimming there. When they are climbing over the rocks, David hurts his foot and can't go on. He is worried because they lose Nina and Mike. When the two return, Nina is very quiet. At home she tells David about a huge saltie at the falls and how scared she was. She apologizes to David. She knows he was right and she was stupid. She asks him not to tell their parents.

**5a) SPEAKING Travelling**
*1* Hi/Hello. What can you see on the Uluru tours, please?
*2* When does the tour start?
*3* How long does the tour take?
*4* Do we get breakfast on the tour?
*5* How much does the tour cost and what do you get for the price?
*6* I'd like to book the tour for tomorrow, for two adults and two students, please.

**5b) SPEAKING Travelling**
**Picture A:**
Picture A shows a scene in the outback with two people, a white camping bus on the right and a small white tent in the foreground on the left. The man is sitting on the front of the camping bus looking at the sky, and the woman is sitting on a camping chair. The sky is bright red, so maybe the sun is going down. There's nothing in the background, only red earth for miles. There's nothing green, no plants or bushes. The people look very relaxed. Maybe they're tired after a hot day of driving. It seems to be very lonely and quiet, maybe even boring. They're both wearing shorts, so it's probably still hot. They've put up the tent before it gets dark.

**Picture B:**
Picture B shows a beach scene in Australia. In the background you see the blue sea and on the left you see the buildings on the other side of the bay. It looks sunny and hot. There are only a few white clouds in the sky. The beach looks clean and bright. It's crowded with people who are enjoying beach life. They're probably laughing and shouting, so the atmosphere must be quite noisy. There are a few tents, but most people are sitting or standing in the sun. In the foreground, in the middle a man and a woman are sitting on the beach. I think maybe the woman is putting sunscreen on the man's arm. Maybe they're thinking that they've had enough sun. They must feel very hot. I don't think that a day on a hot, crowded beach can be very relaxing.

**6 MEDIATION Berlin tours**
Alpha tours – Berlin: tours by bus, bike or on foot, every day; groups – all sizes; modern buses and new bikes; highlights – Brandenburg Gate, Checkpoint Charlie, small part of the Berlin Wall, TV tower, Berlin Cathedral, Charlottenburg Palace and more; tours morning, afternoon and evening, breaks and meal on day tours, guides speak foreign languages, see website for details

# Skills Check 2 Lösungen/Musterlösungen

## 1 LISTENING First day at work

*1* B; *2* A; *3* B; *4* A; *5* B; *6* B; *7* C; *8* A

## 2 READING Jobs

*a)* Young people describing jobs that they do
*b)* *1* D; *2* A; *3* B; *4* F; *5* E
*c)* *1* Nick *2* Sam *3* Lauren *4* Lucy *5* Nick *6* Adam *7* Sam *8* Sam

## 3 WRITING A formal letter

...
Dear Sir/Madam
I read your advertisement in the ... of ... about summer jobs for German-speaking students with the London Tourist Service. I would like to apply and am enclosing my CV in English.
As you can see from my CV, I already have some work experience in Germany. I have a good level of spoken English and I enjoy meeting people and helping customers. I am friendly, reliable and a good team worker.
Could you please answer the following questions? Would your company help with somewhere to stay? What would the working hours be? How much would I earn? I would be able to stay for six weeks.
I look forward to hearing from you.
Yours faithfully ...

## 4 WRITING Your CV

Individual answers. Check with the CVs on pp. 38–39 of your student's book.

## 5 WRITING An informal letter

Hi ...!
I must tell you about an ad that I read today. The London Tourist Service needs German students for summer jobs – and I have applied!
I think working away from home would be good for me – and for my English. But first I want to know more about the jobs, working hours, free time, where I would stay, and so on.
I'd really like to work in London. It would look good on my CV. I might make some new friends and maybe I could visit you in my free time. But maybe the work will be hard, with long hours, bad pay and not much free time ...
I'll let you know if they answer. I'm quite excited!
Love ...

## 6a) SPEAKING Jobs and work experience

**Picture** 1 shows a tourist guide on a London sightseeing bus. Maybe he is telling tourists about the history of the city and its buildings. Maybe the tourists aren't listening to everything he says. I think it's quite a good job because you are mostly outside and you meet a lot of people. But it's the same work every day, like most jobs. The guide probably says exactly the same things to all his tourist groups, and he does the same tour at the same time every day. He probably feels bored, but he always has to be friendly.

**Picture** 2 shows office workers at their computers in a large office. They are probably not very happy. It think it's hard to think and work when there are so many people in one room. There's always some background noise, people telephoning, chatting, walking around, telephones ringing etc. The workers are never private. Everybody sees and hears what they do – the boss too.
I would like to do the job of the tourist guide because I think it's more relaxing. Riding round London in a bus is better than looking at a computer screen all day.

## 6b) SPEAKING Jobs and work experience

I think work experience is important because you learn a lot about the world of work. You have to be punctual, reliable, confident and hard-working. You get to know different kinds of people. You learn skills that are important for your job later, like organisation, telephone skills, team work, maybe new computer skills.
I have some work experience in a book shop and at a petrol station. I liked serving customers and chatting to them. But it was boring at the petrol station between customers. I like to be with people.
I don't have a job at the moment because I have to work hard for school now.
My favourite school subjects are German, English and Maths. I like reading and I am interested in languages. My grades are good too. When I leave school, I'd like to do an interesting apprenticeship, maybe in a bank or in a hotel.

## 7 MEDIATION Small ads

*1* Job in a café: can work 3 hours morning or afternoon, have to work in kitchen and café preparing vegetables, doing tables, serving ice cream and cakes in garden, good pay
*2* Job in hotel (near cathedral): can work part-time or hourly, have to answer phone calls in English and look after foreign guests, needn't have experience of hotel work, above average pay
*3* Job with American family: have to look after young children, afternoons, don't have to do housework, needn't have a driving licence
*4* Job giving English conversation classes: small groups, 2 hours twice a week mornings, don't have to speak German